Walks in the footsteps of
Winston Graham's
POLDARK

Published by Sigma Leisure – an imprint of Sigma Press, Stobart House, Pontyclerc, Penybanc Road, Ammanford, Carmarthenshire SA18 3HP.

British Library Cataloguing in Publication Data
A CIP record for this book is available from the British Library.

ISBN: 978-1-91075-821-2

Typesetting and Design by: Sigma Press, Ammanford.

Cover photographs: © Sue Kittow
main: Polruan; bottom left: Carn Brae Castle; right: Gurnards Head in the distance

Photographs: © Sue Kittow, unless otherwise stated

Maps: © Rebecca Terry
Contains OS data © Crown copyright [and database right] 2016

Printed by: Akcent Media Ltd

Disclaimer: the information in this book is given in good faith and is believed to be correct at the time of publication. No responsibility is accepted by either the author or publisher for errors or omissions, or for any loss or injury however caused. Only you can judge your own fitness, competence and experience. Do not rely solely on sketch maps for navigation: we strongly recommend the use of appropriate Ordnance Survey (or equivalent) maps.

Walks in the footsteps of
Winston Graham's
POLDARK

Sue Kittow

To the dear friends who accompanied me on these walks, pored over maps and helped keep me going throughout a very grim winter (in order of walks walked): Jon and Annie Read, Fiona Sanders, Colin Ivens, Viv Simmons, Mel Bailey, Heather Hosking, Lawson Tickell, Carol Buller, Deb Davis and Rich Milner.

To Moll, for being her.

And to everyone for their ideas, inspiration and encouragement along this journey.

If I have missed anyone out, please forgive me.

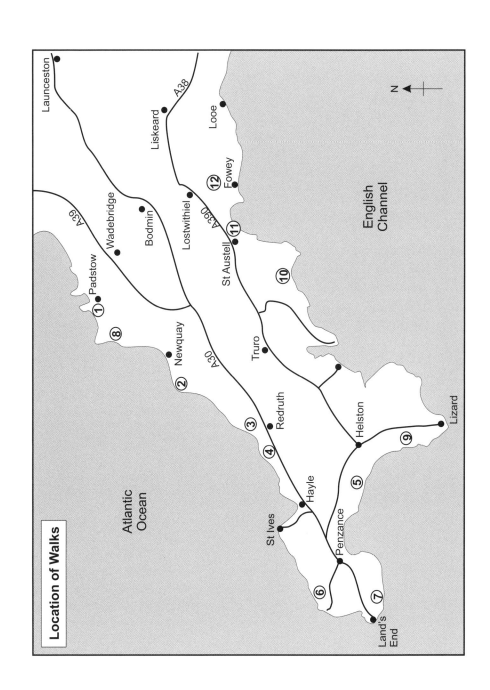

Location of Walks

CONTENTS

INTRODUCTION   9
ACKNOWLEDGEMENTS   12
GENERAL INFORMATION   13

THE WALKS

1. STEPPER POINT   17
    The starting point for the Poldark 2015 TV series

2. PORTH JOKE   28
    The Author's favourite beach

3. ST AGNES AND ST AGNES BEACON   38
    Nampara Valley

4. ILLOGAN   48
    The birthplace of Demelza

5. GODOLPHIN HOUSE   58
    used as Trenwith in the 1970s Poldark series

6. LEVANT AND CROWN ENGINE HOUSES AT BOTALLACK   70
    The mining heart of Poldark

7. PORTHGWARRA AND PORTHCURNO   78
    Scene of the longed for pilchard catch and a daring escape

8. PORTHCOTHAN   90
    Nampara Cove

9. GUNWALLOE   99
    The shipwreck walk

10.. CAERHAYS CASTLE 110
Home of the Trevanion family

11. CHARLESTOWN 121
also known as Truro

12. ST WINNOW AND LERRYN 131
The venue for Dwight Enys and Caroline Penvenen's wedding

INTRODUCTION

I had absolutely no intention of writing another walks book, despite having thoroughly enjoyed writing my second book, *Walks in the Footsteps of Cornish Writers.* The launch party was a great success, and sales of the book have been good, but writing a book gobbles up a huge amount of time and energy that I have to juggle with being a journalist.

But then along came Poldark. And Poldark went global. Living in Cornwall, and breathing every episode, many of us identified with every location, almost became Demelza, and Ross, and all the poor miners – we were swept up in the whole Poldark world. So I pitched the idea of a Poldark Walks book. I figured that if I didn't write it, someone else would, and I couldn't bear that.

As soon as the book was commissioned, I thought, well, I'd better read a few of the Poldark books for research. I had read them before, but a long time ago. I also dug out my old copy of *Poldark's Cornwall,* written by Winston Graham, and got stuck in.

To my amazement, I was hooked from the first book to the last – and there are twelve of them. I had no idea that Winston Graham was so good at writing not only from a man's point of view, but also a woman's. I have learnt so much, not just about Cornish history, and mining history in particular, but about current affairs of the time and worldwide political history. His plots are incredible, as he weaves so many story lines, so deftly, in and out of each chapter, that I have been left gasping as I turn the pages.

His years of working for the Coastguard service during the war gave him ample time to understand the unpredictability of the Cornish weather, most notably the sea, in all her moods. This grew to an even deeper love of Cornwall, and he drew on this to write the Poldark novels.

If you haven't read them, I would urge you to do so for a masterclass in storytelling. He started writing them in the 1940s, then had a 20 year gap when he was writing other novels. During this time he received many letters from fans asking what had happened to his characters. Finally, he was drawn back to the Poldarks – and continued the story.

His style of writing changed over the years, but they still remain page turning novels that have kept me reading far into the night. Although the stories end at the beginning of the 19th century, they manage to seem very contemporary now. Everyone would love an employer – or a husband – like Ross Poldark: just and fair; one of the men, with a strong sense of adventure; not afraid to say – and fight for – what he believes in.

Who wouldn't want a wife or a friend like Demelza? Very much her own woman, despite being deeply in love with Ross – she is witty, down to earth, compassionate, hardworking and intelligent with a dogged optimism that brightens Ross's dark side.

I met Winston Graham when he came to Falmouth for a book signing for *Bella*, his last book. He was in his early nineties then, and my American sister-in-law and I queued in the street, eventually shuffled our way into the bookshop where he signed the books, flirting charmingly with everyone that came along.

That was before the days of selfies, or I would have had one with Winston Graham, Shelagh and myself, grinning at the camera, proudly clutching our copy of *Bella*.

Spin offs are unexpected. I was in St Agnes doing a walk there, and came across a gallery where the artist, Celia Creeper, uses a variety of techniques. She has now created a wonderful series of paintings and posters based on each of my Poldark walks, to be sold alongside them. We could have a joint book launch/exhibition, she suggested. In fact, we will have several.

Another time I received a press release from some publishers saying that Robin Ellis, who played Ross Poldark in the original 1970s TV series, was publishing his third cookbook for diabetics, being one himself. I've ended up writing a piece on his cookbook – which looks so good I will try some recipes myself. You never know who you will meet and how they will impact on your life and your work.

So Poldark has lent yet another aspect to my walks, one that I love and involve my friends in. It's unfortunate that writing this book coincided with the wettest winter for over a hundred years – but that's deadlines for you. I confidently predict that once I have handed the manuscript in, the sun will come out and we will probably have a drought.

Just as I'm always sorry to finish reading a book that I've become emotionally involved in, I was deeply sad to finish writing this one. Having happily immersed myself in Poldark for the last six months, I am now bereft, quietly grieving. Though if the Poldark interest persists, I might be able to write another Poldark walks book....

Sue Kittow
June 2016

ACKNOWLEDGEMENTS

With thanks to my loyal proof readers, in alphabetical order: David Dearlove, Jenny Dearlove, Tony Foster, Av Harcourt, Colin Ivens and Shelagh Smith.

Thanks also to John Roberts for those all important grid references and to Tony Foster for valuable tide and general seagoing information.

GENERAL INFORMATION

- These walks vary in length, so take note according to how much time you have available.

- When out walking, wear appropriate footwear and clothing as weather conditions can change very quickly – rain, fog or even sunshine can descend at a moment's notice.

- Take a mobile phone with you, but be aware that there are many places without a signal, so tell others when and where you are going – and when you return.

- The cliff path is hazardous to dogs who may chase birds and rabbits etc., so keep dogs on a lead near the cliff edge.

- Cornwall is littered with mine shafts, so be careful.

- While the maps contained in this book are as accurate as possible, it is advisable to take the relevant Ordnance Survey map or use one of the OS apps on your phone.

- It's possible you may get lost, or want to just sit and admire the view – take food and water with you, particularly if you have dogs who may get thirsty.

- Respect crops and livestock – keep dogs under control near all animals especially sheep and cattle when their young are with them.

- Respect other people's land and please shut gates behind you.

- Please take all rubbish home with you if you cannot find a litter bin.

- If you are intending to walk on or near beaches, be aware of high and low tides – see following page.

Tides

When walking by the sea it is important to be aware of what the tide is doing. Always check the times of high tide before you set out and know whether it is coming in or going out during your walk. You can find tide times from local radio or in newspapers and many local shops sell tide tables.

The tidal range is much greater at some times than others. Spring tides occur every two weeks around the time of full moon and new moon. The difference between low and high water can be over 5 metres (16ft.) on Cornwall's south coast and 7.5 metres (21ft) on the north coast. Strong on-shore winds can increase the height of tide by up to a metre, especially if accompanied by low atmospheric pressure, usually associated with gales. The time between high and low water is roughly six hours. You are most at risk in the few hours after low water when the tide is returning: it comes in slowly at first but is at its fastest in the 3rd and 4th hours of the flood.

Neap tides, when the range is about half the maximum, occur in the weeks between spring tides. Most tide tables also show the height of high water next to the time – the bigger the number on the day of your walk, the higher the tide will rise.

While we're talking about the sea, just a short word on waves. The complex weather patterns that constantly run into our beautiful Cornish coast often set up wave patterns that cross at an angle to the underlying swell from some distant storm. These will occasionally combine to produce a rogue wave of up to twice the height of the regular waves. There are plenty of clips on-line showing what happens to the reckless when that happens. Don't be one of them!

Below are a few websites you may find helpful.

www.ukho.gov.uk/easytide/EasyTide/ShowPrediction.aspx?PortID=0005&PredictionLength=7
The UK Hydrographic Office is the source of tidal data for all the other sites and limits its free information to the next 7 days.

www.bbc.co.uk/weather/coast_and_sea/tide_tables/10
The BBC list 16 locations around Cornwall and give you a nice little graph of tidal height.

www.newquayweather.com/wxcornishtides.php
Great local weather information. The tides times links you to the UKHO site.

www.cornwalls.co.uk/weather/tide_times.htm
The Cornwall Guide website also provides a wealth of other information for visitors.

www.tidetimes.org.uk/falmouth-tide-times
This site includes an option to order a printed copy of tide tables for the whole year.

WALK ONE
STEPPER POINT

The starting point for the *Poldark* 2015 TV series

Stepper Point's dramatic headland marks the entrance to the sweeping Camel Estuary and Tregirls Beach, both of which feature prominently in the opening episodes of Poldark 2015 and its trailer, with Ross galloping along the cliffs.

In one of the later Poldark novels, *The Four Swans*, young gypsy Emma Tregirls falls in love with one of Demelza's brothers, a preacher. Emma takes her name from Harbour Cove, near Padstow, which is known as Tregirls Beach

Cliffs at Stepper Point

by the locals. The South West Coast Path runs through Tregirls, which at low tide stretches for over half a mile and connects with Hawker's Cove. This innocent looking area becomes the dreaded Doom Bar.

Stepper Point's high cliffs were treacherous for sailing ships that were often becalmed and drifted onto Doom Bar, where they could be rolled over by the breakers. Rockets would fire lines to the shore and capstans were used to haul the ships to safety, but despite this over 600 ships have been wrecked here since the 1800s, and occasionally, one appears from beneath the sand.

Cornwall is not just the setting for the Poldark story: it is one of the main characters, and her unpredictability reflects Ross's stormy personality. Cornwall has many moods – some days wind and rain lash furiously against the cruel cliffs. Gales whistle over the sea, and shriek over Bodmin Moor, its lonely heights lost in low cloud. White horses ride huge Atlantic rollers, tossing unsuspecting yachts petulantly like toys in a bath tub.

Half an hour later, the weather can change to a warm, mischievous breeze, urging us on to have fun – as Ross does. The rugged mining landscape echoes his rugged looks; the brightness of the Cornish light reflects his charm.

When the 2015 Poldark series was filmed, Cornwall was at her most radiant. A million diamonds winked and sparkled on a rich turquoise sea, edged with waves of delicate lace. The statuesque cliffs were dominant towers of strength. The fields and moors wove tapestries of emerald green shot with saffron yellow gorse, and the sky shimmered a cobalt blue, while gulls and buzzards soared effortlessly in the thermals above. In this weather, we forget the months of driving rain, the winter storms that wreck so much. Like a tempestuous relationship, when Cornwall smiles upon us, we forgive everything, for there is no better place to be.

The actors said they felt as if the Poldark story came alive when they arrived in Cornwall. On the day we did this walk, the weather was cold, sulky and quiet, with a slate grey sky reflecting benign green milky waters. A light northerly wind ruffled the surface of the water and our hands and noses started going red.

Directions
From Padstow take the road to Trethillick, continue through Crugmeer until you reach Lelizzick Farm. This is an unmarked road but essentially follow the

What you need to know	
Distance	2½ miles
Allow	2½ hours
Suggested Map	OS Explorer 106 Newquay & Padstow
Starting point	Lellizick Farm; grid reference SW 908774
Terrain	Steep in parts, close to cliff edge in parts
Nearest refreshments	Lellizick Farm in summer or many cafes and restaurants in Padstow
Public transport	The Western Greyhound 555 bus runs regularly between Bodmin and Padstow, via Wadebridge, stopping at Padstow Bus Terminal. For timetable information, visit Traveline or phone 0871 200 22 33
Of interest	Hawker's Cove, the Daymark tower, Coastguard station
Facilities	In Padstow

road on the map from Padstow towards Hawker's Cove. We parked at East Lellizick Farm in a large layby and could have walked through a wooden gate with a picture of a dog on it, that says 'easygoing footpath to Stepper Point' but we opted for the scenic route, and walked down the adjacent road with a 'No Through Road' sign on it.

Having had several disagreements about my map reading skills (which do leave a little to be desired), I entrusted Mr B with the map while we walked, enjoying a fine view of the Camel estuary. Opposite was Brea Hill, which I have often rolled down with my brothers, nephews and nieces, with Trebetherick in the background. We've paddled and swum on Daymer Bay, and walked round the Greenaway to Polzeath where we surfed every year as children. Everything looked different from the other side of the estuary; I'd never walked this section of the coast before.

A fishing boat trundled along the river, trailing a stream of hungry, crying gulls, crescents of white against the grey sky of a cold but still November afternoon. In the distance were the hills of St Austell to the south and Bodmin Moor to the east, while before us lay an astonishing panoramic view of the

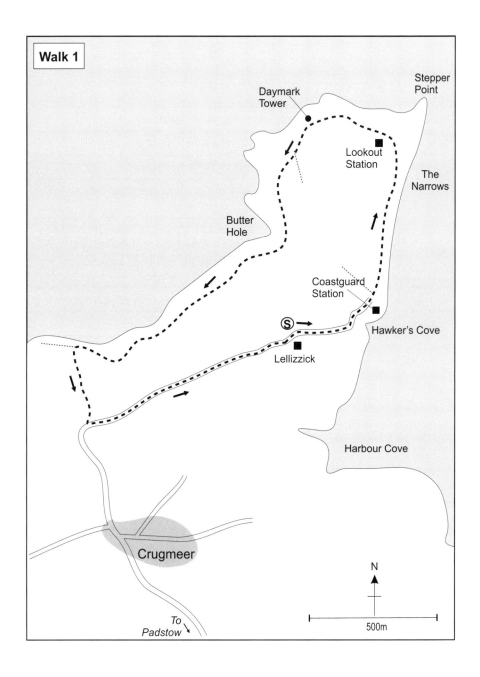

Walk 1

Stepper Point

Daymark Tower

Lookout Station

The Narrows

Butter Hole

Coastguard Station

Hawker's Cove

Lellizzick

Harbour Cove

Crugmeer

N

To Padstow

500m

View down Camel estuary

Camel Estuary as it wound away towards Padstow and Rock, leaving gaps of enticing yellow sandy beaches. "We should come back here in the summer; there are some lovely coves," mused Mr B.

The first Padstow lifeboat, built by the Padstow Harbour Association, was stationed here, before the local branch of the RNLI was formed in 1855. In 1931 a new boathouse was built, and a roller slipway, but by 1967 silting up became a problem and the lifeboat was moved to Trevose Head, a few miles to the west.

Walking past a row of fishermen's cottages, we continued towards Hawker's Cove past the old coastguard station that is now a house, and a sign saying 'Slow Please, Deaf Cat'. We followed the coastpath towards Trevose Head, which led past tamarisk trees, and turned right by a public footpath sign to 'Trevone Bay 3¼ miles via Stepper Point'. The path winds down past some cottages and a tiny cove with a boat moored up, while the water lapped quietly below us. Bright yellow and orange nasturtium grew in abundance here, the colours a welcome cheer against the greyness of a winter's day, and we passed a little wooden dog's kennel with 'Kevin' written on it, followed by a vibrant picture of a cross looking chicken, with a notice saying 'Free Range Chickens. Please keep dog on lead'.

With Moll duly restrained, we passed a few stone cottages below us, and walked through a wooden kissing gate by Hawker's Cove (grid reference SW912776). The waves lapped below us, looking very Mediterranean, as we continued along a well trodden part of the coastal footpath.

Looking out across the estuary, at low tide the sand on this side of the water extends almost to Doom Bar. According to Cornish folklore, the Mermaid of Padstow fell in love with a local lad named Tom Yeo, who mistook her for a seal (or so he said), and shot her. They do say that hell hath no fury like a woman scorned, and in this instance, she provoked a massive storm which wrecked all the ships in the harbour. Not satisfied with that, she threw a huge sandbar across the river to endanger all future sailors venturing in.

Glad that we were safely on dry land, we noticed a derelict building that Mr B fell in love with – some crumbled remains, with a pigeon perched on top. While he walked on, indulging in visions of turning it into a dream dwelling, I turned my eye to the plump, healthy lichen on the gnarled bushes round

Trevose headland

here, and an abundance of glossy ivy. The last of the bracken was in evidence here, turned a jaundiced yellow in places, unlike the crunchy crisp brown of its cousins on the south coast.

Birds were in abundance today: a robin chirped at us as we walked past, then later on we saw a joyous parcel of linnets, a few blackbirds and a chaffinch or two. Pipits and red-throated divers have also been spotted here at this time of year.

There's a stream running down the middle of the rocky path here, so wear waterproof boots! The path became quite steep and a sure test of our fitness, judging by Mr B's breathing and my legs. On our left we saw a slate quarry of rich, dark purple stone, while down on the cliffs to our right crouched a couple of black backed gulls and below them, two cormorants, their alert heads turning this way and that, on the lookout for the next meal.

At the next gate was a notice advising that sheep graze in this area, so please keep dogs on leads. The waves crashing on the opposite shore, a mile away, were a distant rumble, like a train approaching, while ahead of us we could see a group of rocks known as Rainer and King Philip rocks, and, over to our right, Pentire Point, past Polzeath.

Coming to a wooden stile, we clambered over to spectacular views, and a path that led to Stepper Point, but we decided to take a detour up to the Lookout station which was opened in 2000. Here, Richard Oakley welcomed us and noted us in his logbook – as he does all walkers in winter, in case people disappear or have an accident. He pointed out the part of the cliffs where they filmed Ross cantering along the path, with the sleek promontory of Trevose Head glimmering in the distance to the south west.

The history of Doom Bar and the many shipwrecks were detailed here on a map dated 1839. The Daymark is a chimney-like tower standing on the cliff edge, to the west of the station, and was built in 1830 of stone and limewashed. It's 40 ft high and at 240 ft above sea level is visible from 20 miles away. The purpose was to make the entrance to Padstow less hazardous during daylight hours, thereby preventing more ships being wrecked in this area: 96 vessels were lost between 1800 and 1826. The Daymark cost £29 to build and the money was raised by giving the donors voting rights in the Harbour Association. One guinea would buy one vote.

Daymark tower

I could just imagine a ship, in Poldark's time, labouring to get round the headland against a foul tide before darkness fell. The villagers waiting anxiously to see if there would be a wreck – which would mean food or possibly coal, for their families. Anything to help miners' meagre wages.

We continued along this path, turning right to reach the Daymark tower (or Pepper Pot), passing puffballs and toadstools as we walked. Archaeologists have found flint tools on the headland which indicate that people lived in this part of Stepper Point as far back as 6,000 years ago, and possibly even earlier. The views from the tower are incredible – the long, low headland of Trevose, like a dragon's body barely emerging from the sea, with Gulland Rock looming in the distance.

The turf was smooth and bouncy, like a golf course, as we walked along, making for easy walking, and in the distance the cliffs undulated like steep folds on a green blanket. Far below us were the hollow booms from caves carved out by the sea – sometimes these caves collapse, leaving a sinkhole, as can be seen by Pepper Hole, Butter Hole and Fox Hole along this part of the coast – Roundhole Point, over to the south, is another example of this erosion.

Skirting round the edge of Butter Hole, the first of these massive craters, we encountered a field of bullocks which made me nervous so I put Moll on the lead and hurried on, while Mr B leapt around cheerfully taking photographs. We followed the path round the edge of the cliffs, through another kissing gate and a waymark sign at the top of the hill.

There was a boggy part here, but Moll scampered ahead looking like a cross between a manic rabbit and a muddy sheep. Waves crashed noisily against the teeth of the cliffs, leaving toothpaste trails of jetsam that spread lazily over the water. Gulls nested in crooks on the cliffs while others soared overhead carving graceful arcs in the sky.

Over a stile we climbed, noticing the austere farmland on our left, and arrived at another kissing gate where we found a map on a gatepost that indicated we weren't where Mr B thought we were at all. So it's not just me that can't read maps, then.

As we were running out of daylight, we decided to take a slightly shorter route than planned and walked along to the next viewpoint where we turned left, and followed a Cornish stone wall along the left hand side of the field. The

Sinkholes

views from here are spectacular, over Harlyn Bay, then Cataclews Point and Mother Ivey's Bay. We walked along the middle of the field back to the road, where we turned left and walked back on the road we'd driven in on.

As we got back to the van, church bells were ringing from a nearby valley. We couldn't see the church – maybe it was St Enodoc's, where, in the first Poldark series, Rowella Chynoweth gets her way and marries Arthur Solway. This is a 13th century church that, until fairly recently, was mostly covered in sand. In 1851 when Bishop Philpotts visited, he had to climb in through the roof because the sands were higher than the east gable, the pews were worm eaten and the roof and belfry were inhabited by bats. It has since been restored and is a beautiful church, well worth a visit, with incredible views – and the resting place of Sir John Betjeman.

Finally we arrived back at Lellizick Farm, which offers B&B and cream teas in the summer. As it was winter, we headed back to Padstow and enjoyed a cup of tea there, before strolling along the harbour and returning home.

Winston Graham used many events in Cornish history and wove them into his storylines. He was clearly bewitched by Cornwall, and made a point of getting to know it very well, in all its moods and quirks. He understood the different types of landscape, as well as the people that lived in them – the fishermen, the miners and the older people, as gnarled as the landscape that shaped them. All of this is reflected in his characters.

This is what informed Poldark, and made the books and the television series so vital, so real and so compelling. The books haven't dated and the success of the ongoing TV series proves the enduring popularity of the characters and their stories.

PORTH JOKE

The Author's favourite beach

Winston Graham said, "It is the business of the novelist – or should be – to show both sides (of humanity). If in the Poldarks I have tended to show too much of the warmer side, that is my own fault – or my own truth". Porth Joke was one of the author's favourite places (mine too) that on a sunlit day shows very much the glorious, raw warm beauty of Cornwall, but visit it in a storm and you will see the dark and cruel side of Cornwall, stripped bare. The name Porth Joke is thought to be derived from the Cornish *Pol-Lejouack* meaning Jackdaw cove.

Porth Joke

It was this area, from Pentire to Crantock Bay and round West Pentire to Porth Joke (known as Polly Joke to locals), that helped make up an overall picture of Nampara in the Poldark novels. This was also where the author spent so much of his time absorbing and noting the moods of the sea, the birds and the many and varied wild flowers. He came to this area – in particular West Pentire – many times as a boy before the Second World War, and later he would walk here with his fiancee planning the honeymoon that never happened on account of the war.

I can imagine them walking hand in hand across the firm fine sand, while warm ripples of waves splashed around their bare feet. They might have climbed over the rocks, as we have, pointing out sea anemones and limpets; nesting gulls and swooping gannets, while the waves crashed against the cliffs, spitting Atlantic tears as they fell.

Directions
At Chiverton Cross roundabout, take the A3075 to Newquay and continue through Goonhavern until you reach a small left hand turn signposted West

What you need to know	
Distance	4 miles
Allow	2½ hours
Suggested Map	OS Explorer 104 Redruth & St Agnes
Starting point	National Trust car park Cubert Common; grid reference SW 776599
Terrain	Several steep hills
Nearest refreshments	Holywell Bay – Treguth Arms or cafes in summer
Public transport	587 bus to Holywell Bay; nearest train station is Newquay, 4 miles away
Of interest	Polly Joke; Holywell Bay; Barrow at Cubert Common; Kelsey Head
Facilities	Toilets at Holywell Bay; both beaches are dog friendly year round. Golf course at Holywell Bay Parking at Cubert Common £2 at time of walking

Pentire and Crantock. After Crantock village, follow the signs to West Pentire, then turn left at a sign to Treago Farm campsite. Head down the hill, past Treago Farm and onto a rough track over Cubert Common. At the end of this, passing through several five barred gates, is a National Trust car park at Cubert Common which is the start of the walk.

It's several years since Viv and I did walks together for publication, as she had to be in London for a few years, then on returning to Cornwall, broke her ankle, so this was her first long walk for a while, and I was aware of having to treat her gently. But the weather was on our side. After what seemed like months of dull grey, wet weather, the clouds parted and the sun shone. This was my late husband's favourite beach, as well as Winston Graham's, and I have happy memories of many visits to Polly Joke.

Today we left the car park and – as the author may well have done – headed down towards the sea, past a noticeboard detailing walks around Crantock, Cubert and Holywell. The path here is sandy and was muddy today, but sheltered by high hawthorn hedges on our right, beyond which lay sun-kissed fields, and the grassy slopes of Cubert Common on our left.

Polly Joke beach

"Here, I made us some rock buns," said Viv, producing a plastic bag full of the goodies. I thanked her with some caution – her last lot of rock buns won first prize in a village show but there were no other entries and not even the judges would eat them. This batch, however, were packed full of dried fruit and – er – mincemeat. "Left over from my mince pies," she said cheerfully. Whatever it was, they tasted good and cheered the walk even more.

Further on, we noted a stream far down in the valley on our right – one day we encountered a cow that had wandered down there for a drink, but today it was quiet save the ripple and swish of the water rushing down to the sea. We had our first glimpse of Polly Joke here, through the hawthorn trees – a narrow slice of navy blue rumpled cloak with multitudinous white specks, edged by huge waves of ermine.

Passing through a gate, the path opened out, with sun lighting up the fields dotted with hawthorn bushes on our right, and the continuation of Cubert Common on our left. The rumble of the sea grew louder as we walked, until we emerged onto sand dunes and a sign pointing left saying 'Holywell 2 miles' and 'West Pentire and Crantock' to the right. But first we took time to enjoy

Approaching Kelsey Head

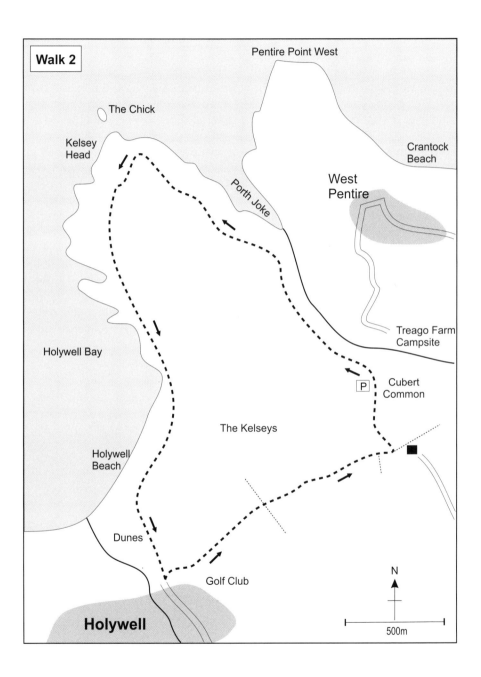

Walk 2

Pentire Point West

The Chick

Kelsey
Head

Crantock
Beach

Porth Joke

West
Pentire

Treago Farm
Campsite

Holywell Bay

P Cubert
Common

The Kelseys

Holywell
Beach

Dunes

Golf Club

N

500m

Holywell

a run along the beach, crossing the bridge over the stream bisecting the sand. Polly Joke is still unspoilt. There are, thankfully, no ice cream vans or kiosks, no toilets, no cafes, just pure pale gold Cornish sand and, occasionally, a herd of cattle that meander across the sand, to the astonishment of the many visitors that appear in summer. The 10-15 minute walk from the car park puts off some of the lesser able beach goers, as do the lack of facilities, but this is a popular beach for surfers, families who enjoy rock pools and natural pools safe for bathing, and it is sheltered from northerly winds by the high, jagged cliffs trimmed with tamarisk trees.

The main path towards Holywell is westwards, to the left, but we opted to head across the beach and clamber up some rocks to reach the headland, which is steeper but shorter. A south easterly wind blew our cobwebs away as we followed the footpath round Kelsey Head, taking in the view of the rock named The Chick, out to sea, and Pentire Point over to the North East on our right.

We descended some steps, over a boardwalk, relishing the rare sunshine, as were many other walkers out today, and stopped to watch the Atlantic rollers crashing against the rocks – a pastime that can happily consume hours, marvelling at the majestic power of nature.

Kelsey Head

I have often walked round towards Pentire and Crantock, but never round Kelsey Head, and wasn't disappointed. The walking is easy here, over springy turf and the headland is used by many nesting seabirds such as the common tern, plover, black-headed gull, which can be seen in spring.

We followed the signs pointing round the headland until eventually we saw the wide expanse of Holywell Bay, and its cluster of houses nestled inland. Out to sea we noticed the Carters or Gull Rocks looming out of the water like giant sharks' teeth.

It was incredibly windy the day we did this walk, but this has to be one of the loveliest parts of the coast, even in gale force winds. Finally we reached Holywell Bay, much larger and more dramatic than I'd remembered, with over a mile of glistening sand at low tide, and numerous walkers enjoying the beach with their dogs.

After several false starts, and suffering a deluge, we finally found the correct route which is to walk half way along the beach, then turn left along a path through the massive sand dunes which lead to a bridge at the far end of the beach.

Holywell and Gull Rocks

"Can I have another rock bun?" I bleated, blood sugar levels having plummeted on the way round. Viv doled out another bun and, energy restored, we set off along a metalled track in search of a cup of tea.

The track led us past some shops, then we turned left towards Holywell Bay village, past the beautifully named Rhubarb Hill, and on our left we found the Treguth Arms, a lovely 13th century pub with a very welcome woodburner. There we were greeted royally and warmed ourselves with cups of coffee for us and biscuits for the dogs.

On the wall in the pub was a picture of Treguth Farm 1900 looking towards the beach at Holywell Bay. "Note the lack of dunes at this point – the dunes at Holywell Bay are the product of only the last 60-80 years." And sure enough – there were no dunes in 1900, which made me wonder if they had been around in Winston Graham's day – had he or his family walked through them or tumbled down them in the sunshine?

Suitably refreshed and warmed, we left the warm pub with some regret, but we only had about 45 minutes of daylight left, so felt we should find our way back to Polly Joke. From the pub we headed back down the road and past Rhubarb Hill, we turned right by the Holywell stores. Further along was a No Through Road sign and a Public Footpath sign to Treguth Common.

We walked through the dunes, keeping the houses on our right, following the advice of another dog walker who looked at us askance when we said we needed to get back to Polly Joke. "You've got a bit of a walk," she said grimly, and we wondered whether we would actually reach there in daylight.

The last of the sun lit the dunes ahead of us as we walked, taking a right hand fork through the dunes with a wire fence on the left, and a waymark sign pointing ahead. Reaching the golf course, we took the left hand path, leaving the golf course on our right, and climbed up a very steep hill, Viv pausing to catch her breath, while a rainbow lit up the sky ahead of us. Through a kissing gate, where the path levelled out, was a signpost to Crantock.

Finally we could see Crantock ahead, and the Kelseys to our left, showing the path we walked around earlier. We were now on Cubert Common, an agricultural common and Site of Special Scientific Interest that houses a massive barrow on the far southern edge of the common, which is now owned by the National Trust. It is probable that the barrow was built for an important local burial, for there is a wonderful view of the sea from here. From early spring this open grassland is studded with primrose, cowslips, squill and yellow flag iris, while skylarks soar and twitter overhead. Today it was quiet as the sun set, the only sound the distant rumble of the waves crashing off Kelsey Head.

The path continued through another a kissing gate, a dip, then over a new bridge over a stream and another kissing gate and headed diagonally over the common. Looking ahead, to our right, we saw a big house with three tall chimneys and headed slightly right, towards the house. At another kissing gate we turned right and this brought us to the path that leads from the car park down to Polly Joke.

We reached here just as the moon appeared in the sky, and I wondered how many times Winston Graham had wandered these paths, paddling in the seas here and swimming in the surf while he thought up the next plot line in the Poldark books.

He wrote the first four Poldark books between 1945 and 1953, and never intended to write any more. But a steady stream of letters over the years requested that he did. His style of writing changed over those years: it's easy to discern a less romantic, sharper tone. He had also had considerable success with his suspense novels, several of which had been made into films (*The Walking Stick, Marnie, Angell, Pearl and Little God*). There was no reason for him to return to Poldark.

Winston Graham was also away from Cornwall during this period of his life. He says he doesn't know why he decided to revisit the Poldark novels, but in 1971 he did. However, he found it extremely difficult to pick up the characters, the plot lines, the situations and carry on. He said he didn't dare read the first four books in case that put him off, but he did dip into the books and was amazed at how much came rushing back: it was as if the characters were merely asleep, waiting to wake up and be written about again.

The first hundred pages were the worst, and after that the stories took on a life of their own, he said. And from then on, with a few exceptions, he wrote only Poldark for the rest of his life.

I first came to Polly Joke twenty years ago. My late husband made jewellery out of tin from South Crofty, the last working mine in Cornwall, and one windswept winter day we came here to bury some treasure (a pendant made of tin) near one of the tamarisk trees by the coastal footpath. He liked the idea of burying treasure in places that he loved, and whenever I go I try and remember under which tamarisk tree we buried it. I'm never quite sure, but that doesn't matter – if anyone should find it, one day, I know he would be delighted. I have often returned, for Polly Joke reminds me of how beaches used to be when I was young: wild and unspoilt, yet peaceful and secluded.

After the war, Winston Graham brought his wife here and they found the area covered in brambles and barbed wire, but otherwise untouched. And so they continued to return, for the rest of their lives. Once you've been, you'll see why. It is a place that touches the soul, just as the Poldark books do.

WALK THREE
ST AGNES AND ST AGNES BEACON
Nampara Valley

This area was the lifeblood of Winston Graham, who lived and wrote close by at Perranporth, however the Nampara Lodge Hotel, 4 St Michael's Road, was sadly pulled down in 2004 due to ground subsidence. The area round St Agnes is used in the 2015 TV series as the Nampara Valley, part of Ross Poldark's estate, and the area off Beacon Drive in St Agnes is used in the finale of the series, when Ross is arrested by soldiers for looting from the shipwrecks and inciting riots.

Mining runs through the Poldark books like a rich vein of ore – albeit one that runs thin at times, causing Ross and others to go heavily into debt. St Agnes – or Sawle in the books – was a mining community from the 16th century until the 1920s, when there were over 100 copper and tin mines in the area, employing up to 1000 miners, whose wives and children also worked on the surface.

As Winston Graham says in *Poldark's Cornwall,* "Nampara means 'valley of bread'. It is an extraordinary coincidence that this tiny district of Perranporth, before the Great Western Railway built its line there and effaced local landmarks, was renowned for its bakery. Yet the name goes back centuries."

When Ross arrives back at Nampara on his return from America, his love of the land is striking. He thinks about the Wheal Grambler mine, which provided the subsistence for not just the Poldark family, but for over 300 miners and their families. As he rides past the old, familiar mine workings of Wheal Maiden, where he played as a boy, he feels he's finally returned home. The Mellingey stream mutters "like an old woman" and "There ahead in the soft and sighing darkness was the solid line of Nampara House... smaller than he remembered, lower and more squat: it straggled like a row of workmen's cottages."

The Nampara Valley is Ross's sanctuary. Ever the adventurer, his life takes him to many distant shores, but it is to Nampara, and to Demelza, that he always returns. This is his heart and soul, and without it he could not exist. For Demelza too, this becomes her home and she loves and cherishes the garden, the animals and Nampara Cove, running down there to fish and swim. For Ross and Demelza, home could never be anywhere else.

What you need to know	
Distance	2½ miles approximately
Allow	1½ hours
Suggested Map	OS Explorer 104 Redruth & St Agnes
Starting point	Car park in the centre of St Agnes; grid reference SW 719504
Terrain	Steep in parts, also rocky
Nearest refreshments	Plenty of cafes at St Agnes or Chapel Porth cafe
Public transport	A variety of buses serve St Agnes: www.cornwallpublictransport.info/bus_timetables.asp Nearest train station is Truro, 10 miles away
Of interest	Bronze Age barrow; Wheal Coates mine buildings; remains of Cameron training camp
Facilities	Nearest toilets St Agnes or Chapel Porth

Directions

From Truro, take the A390 then at Chiverton Cross, take the 2nd exit onto the B3277. At the roundabout take the 3rd exit and stay on the B3277. At the next roundabout take the second exit onto Vicarage Road and you are in St Agnes.

Drive through the village, and soon you will see a car park up on the left near the library where there is an honesty box. From the car park walk back down the hill until you come to the road and turn right. Past the Railway Inn, Mr B and I continued until we came to a mini roundabout, then took the turning on the right, up Goonvrea Road, which is signposted towards the Beacon. Walking along this road for about 5 minutes, we came to a Public Footpath sign to the Beacon on our right and walked up here.

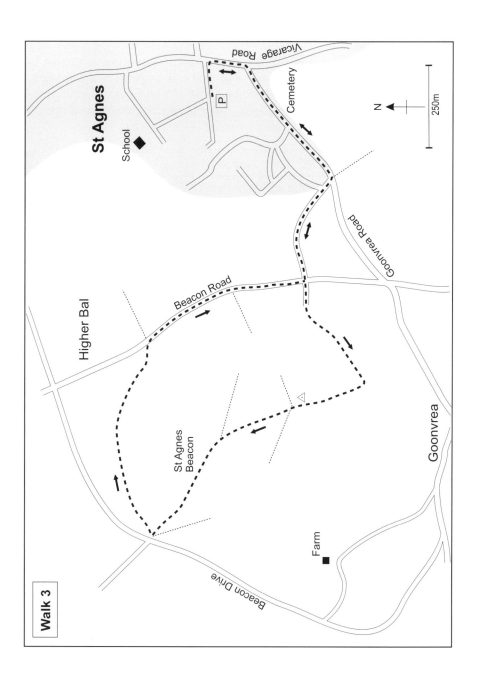

Walk 3

We then came to the junction with Beacon Road, and continued across it with another Public Footpath sign pointing up towards the Beacon. We walked up a rough tarmac drive with hedges on either side, and a field dotted with crows and black cattle.

The beacon rose up in front of us, covered in a rough brown duvet of end of season bracken as we passed Beacon Farm Cottages; a row of what would have been miners' cottages (straight out of Poldark) with tiny square porches and tubs of bright pink cyclamen and miniature purple pansies to lend some colour to the greyness of a November morning.

Looking down the hill, we had a good view of St Agnes and its patchwork of fields, allotments and a few young planted trees. Beacon Farm came next, with a wild garden and teasel peeking over the hedges while a few ponies grazed in the fields.

This track leads to an open field with lush grass which Moll scampered over with delight – "She loves the grass beneath her feet," observed Mr B, as Moll did an exuberant somersault. We climbed over a stile and onto the Beacon,

Heading up the Beacon

looking over to Porthtowan and Portreath beaches in front of us to the south west, and on the skyline Carn Brae, Four Lanes television mast, the silhouette of the old arsenic works at Poldice; and Nancecuke, the chemical defence site at Portreath.

Down below snuggled Towanroath engine house of Wheal Coates (Wheal means mine in Cornish) which has been lovingly restored by the National Trust and has graced the pages of many a book, including Daphne du Maurier's *Vanishing Cornwall;* some say it is the most photographed engine house of all. The earliest reference to the mine is in 1692, but the building was erected in 1872 to house a pumping engine needed to keep Wheal Coates mine free of water. Tin and copper was mined here between 1820 and 1914 and the copper can still be seen as blue streaks in the surrounding stone.

Here you may see lumps of pockmarked porous granite, threaded with veins of cassiterite, and spots of haematite; proof of the rich mining heritage of this area. The grey day was not lifted by any colourful growth, but finally we saw a single common knapweed, some gorse blooms, confusingly next to bramble flowers – a true sign of the winter confusion this year.

View towards Porthtowan

Wheal Coates *photograph: C Buller*

We continued walking until we reached a junction of several paths: we took the steep one leading directly up to the Beacon, or rather, Mollie and I did, while Mr B scampered around taking photographs. There was a stiff south westerly wind blowing, which increased as we reached the top until I could barely stand up, but the view from the trig point on top is utterly breathtaking, with North Cornwall laid before us like a magical map.

Triangulation stations, or trig points, were typically marked by a small pillar and installed by the Ordnance Survey to facilitate the original detailed surveys of the country. Because of GPS, trig points are now almost obsolete and some are being removed, though apparently people can adopt these posts to look after them. For those without much sense of direction – and I include myself in this – the trig point has a very helpful diagram of places of interest, distances and directions.

St Agnes Beacon is a granite outcrop with Bronze Age barrows on the summit, where bonfires are lit on Midsummer Eve and other special occasions. Several million years ago, this beacon was an island and mining evidence shows that there was a pebbly beach at about the same height as today's ground level.

View from The Beacon

Now the old sea floor shoreline is covered in thick layers of china clay which is extracted in the Newdown Sand and Clay Pits, further along the road.

On a clear day it is possible to see 30 church spires or towers, but not today, with rain clouds looming. However, from the highest point of 192 metres (628 feet) we could see westwards to St Ives, shrouded in mist, and up to Trevose Head near Padstow in the north east. We could just make out the 'Cornish Alps' – the china clay tips of St Austell in the distance to the east and, nearer, the granite outcrop of Carn Brea to the south. Down below us was Wheal Kitty, and we could just glimpse Falmouth on the opposite coast, slightly east of south.

Having admired the view for rather longer than I would have liked, given the howling wind and dropping temperatures, we descended on the path heading towards the sea, looking a motley collection: Mr B was wearing his white and black striped sunhat (in lieu of a hood, given the forecast rain) and my hands had started turning blue: never a good, or attractive sign. "Hang on," ordered Mr B, pulling both sleeves down over my frozen hands and securing the sleeves so I couldn't use my fingers. Next he tied my hood tightly and wrapped me up so I looked as if I was setting out on an Arctic exhibition.

At a fork we took the path going slightly to the right, among springy beds of heather, now turned off-white. From spring into late summer, this heathland is ablaze with deep rich saffron-yellow gorse and the vivid purple of the heather.

In spring, the headlands and turf areas have wonderful displays of the blue star-like flowers of squill (St Agnes Head is an excellent spot for this), as well as splashes of yellow from the bacon and egg (trefoil) and dyer's greenweed. Yellow kidney vetch also flowers here, as well as sea campion and rock rose.

It was too cold for us to see lizards, slow worms and adders but we did spot a few ravens and a stonechat with its chirpy distinctive voice. If you're lucky you may also see fulmars and peregrines, and we saw a few buzzards soaring over the cliffs, searching for prey. With those large birds, I always keep a close eye on Moll, just in case one was extra hungry and fancied a snack.

As we descended, following the winding path, each step revealed another part of the panoramic view; even on an overcast day, this walk is well worth doing to appreciate North Cornwall at its best.

We took another right hand fork, still walking towards the sea, looking out on Bawden Rocks – otherwise known as Man and his Man. "We need to head back towards St Agnes," said Mr B, whose sense of direction is better than mine."There should be a path leading round the bottom of the Beacon."

Fortunately, at this point we reached a lone walker named Brian who is a local of these parts and very helpful as well as knowledgeable. "If you look down there," said Brian, pointing towards the lower part of the Beacon on the seaward side, "that's where Ross was arrested at the end of the (2015) series." He laughed. "Although he would have been able to see the soldiers coming from half a mile away – there's no way soldiers could creep up on him as it's so exposed."

Pointing uphill, Brian continued, "This was an encampment for the Cameron training camp for the 100th Light Anti-Aircraft battery. They had targets here and they used to shoot at them. One of my aunts got to know a Canadian GI and at the end of the war she had to decide whether to go back to Canada with him or stay – she eventually went!"

From 1943-44 the camp housed army units of various nationalities prior to embarkation to France. After the war, the bungalows provided accommodation for local families until more council houses were built.

Pointing down to what looked like a pond full of sand, Brian told us that this was very fine foundry sand used for casting which had been blown over the land over many years. "I always thought it was a raised beach, but it's not," he said.

Following Brian's directions, we found a small path on our right which wound round the bottom of the Beacon, heading north towards St Agnes. We were out of the wind here, which was a relief, and able to take in the chequered fields below us, studded with ponies, while a few crows stalked up and down the grass like indignant, patrolling soldiers. The industrial landscape of mine chimneys lay below us, showing how important mining was in Poldark times. Hundreds of lives depended on the copper and tin mines, but those lives were often short owing to malnutrition, poverty and many hours working in the dark, cramped stifling heat underground.

The miles of Perranporth beach lay some distance to the north east ahead of us (Hendrawna in the Poldark books) with Ligger Point at the end of the beach, then Carter's or Gull Rocks just off Penhale Point, and further in the distance is Chick Rock off Kelsey Head. Today, waves smashed against the cliffs in a frothy tantrum, with spume exploding in outrage. No wonder ships were wrecked so often; no wonder the Cornish have always had a healthy respect for the sea.

Wading through a boggy part, glad that I was wearing my boots, we passed swathes of arthritic, brittle bracken, a bay tree, and the last of the campion. Passing a St Agnes Beacon National Trust sign on our right, the path wound round another huge bay tree and we arrived back at Beacon Road.

From here you can cross the road, over a stone stile and walk across fields to the village – there are several paths up to the Beacon and down into the village of St Agnes, so don't worry if you miss one. Like buses, another will come along soon. But for the purposes of this walk, we turned right and continued along Beacon Road until we came to the footpath we'd walked up on the way here, and retraced our steps.

Cow parsley still lined the hedges here, despite it being November, and the sweet musty smell of an autumn bonfire drifted over the fields.

Standing by any trig point always makes me feel as if I'm on top of the world, but this one has a special feeling to it, in my mind. Perhaps because I'm

North Cornwall view *photograph: C Buller*

imagining Ross being arrested by the red coat soldiers (this only happened in the TV series, not the books, in case you're confused). Or perhaps because, when I read the books, I can see Ross and Demelza walking over the gorse-flamed moorland, or cantering along the cliffs with Garrick lolloping alongside, or chasing rabbits as Moll was doing today. I can see Wheal Coates, and imagine what life was like when the mine engines were working; see the miners arriving and departing from work, walking along these very paths. This, to me, is their stamping ground. They're so near you can almost touch them. Look closer and you can see them. This is their home.

WALK FOUR
ILLOGAN
The birthplace of Demelza

Demelza Carne was born in Illogan, a small mining town near Redruth, where she helped raise her six brothers after the death of their mother. Ross comes across Demelza at Redruth Fair, where her dog is being taunted by locals. He rescues her and discovers that she is not only starving but badly beaten by her miner father. Ross offers her a job as housemaid at Nampara which she gladly accepts, as long as her dog, Garrick, can come too.

At first she finds it difficult to live in such unaccustomed luxury, though doesn't think much of having to be clean, and manages to smuggle Garrick into the house. But she knows how fortunate she is to be away from the poverty, filth and brutality of her family, and develops into a loyal, empathetic and amusing companion, who works hard to earn her place not only in the house, but eventually in Ross's affections. She is the very opposite of Elizabeth, Ross's first love, who married his cousin, Francis: while Demelza is earthy, brave and loyal, Elizabeth is fragile, indecisive and highly strung. Ross can see how much easier life is with Demelza around, and begins, cautiously, to experience moments of happiness.

In the first book, Ross Poldark, and the 2015 TV series, Demelza's father and two of his brothers come to Nampara to take Demelza home, accusing Ross of stealing her. A posse of Illogan miners accompany them, as backup – "an army against one man. That's brave," observes Ross wryly. A fight ensues, and although Ross takes on the three men, he wins. The Illogan miners are no match for Ross's mining friends, and soon they, too, retreat, leaving the inhabitants of Nampara battered but quietly victorious.

Demelza is highly relieved that she can stay at Nampara: she realises how much she loves Ross, and the couple become lovers, but afterwards she feels she has put him in an impossible situation. Broken hearted, she prepares to return to Illogan, but Ross comes after her, and to her delight, insists that they marry. The neighbours are astonished.

Tehidy Woods are famous around the Illogan area for walks but also for live outdoor theatre. This walk takes in a route that Demelza may well have taken with her brothers when she needed to escape her father's drunken beatings.

What you need to know	
Distance	3 miles approximately
Allow	1¾ hours
Suggested Map	OS Explorer 104, Redruth & St Agnes
Starting point	Alexandra Road; grid reference SW 671435
Terrain	Mostly flat - easy going
Nearest refreshments	Illogan – Robartes Arms, The Cornish Oven pasty shop
Public transport	Public Transport Buses 46, 47. Nearest railway station Redruth
Of interest	Tehidy park; Manningham Woods and house; Illogan churchyard
Facilities	Nearest toilets are Robartes Arms, Illogan or Portreath for nearest public toilets

Directions

From the A30, Heather, Carol, MollieDog and I took the exit signed for Redruth and followed the signs to Camborne and Pool (A3047). Staying on this road, we passed the Camborne/Redruth hospital on the left, then a garage on the right and took the second right, signed Chariot Road. At the end of this is a crossroads at Paynters Lane End, and then a left turn into Alexandra Road.

We parked at the end of Alexandra Road, near the Cornish Oven pasty shop (there are no parking restrictions on this road). It was a cool, crisp January afternoon as we walked back to the crossroads, opposite a Co-op corner shop and the Robartes Arms and turned left through some black wrought iron gates into Manningham Wood.

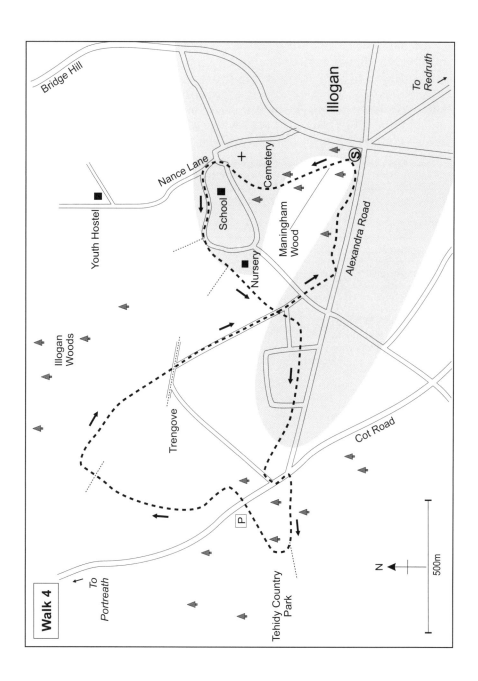

Walk 4

Bridge Hill

Illogan

To Redruth

Youth Hostel

Nance Lane

Cemetery

School

Maningham Wood

Alexandra Road

Nursery

Illogan Woods

Trengove

Cot Road

P

To Portreath

Tehidy Country Park

N

500m

This was originally an ornamental amenity area for Manningham House in the 1700s with a semi-natural plantation containing non-native species. After decades of the land being a wilderness behind locked and rusted gates, a nature trail was created in 2004 which is now disabled/wheelchair/pram friendly. Leaflets for the nature trail can be obtained from any of the local shops.

Passing several carved statues, we meandered our way along the nature trail, noting young hazel and hawthorn trees, together with other native species of plants. Coming to a large carved wooden seat, with a huge acorn in the middle, we followed the path round to the right, then turned left, passing another seat. This leads to Illogan church with the modern cemetery on our right, while jackdaws called to each other in the trees on our left.

Heading towards Illogan church, *Pesvner Architectural Guides* states that "although Illogan parish was the centre of Cornish mining, the church is in entirely rural surroundings". Things have changed a lot since then, as it is now surrounded by houses and there is a planning application to build more houses on the land next to the cemetery.

In Demelza's time, however, the few houses would have been on the far side of the church. Before the path turned to the right, we glimpsed Manningham House on the left, which was the old rectory for the 17th century church, and is now a Grade 2 listed private house. It was built in 1880-85 in Bath stone by Lord de Dunstanville of the Basset family. The position of rector would have been given to a son of an aristocratic family, so John Basset was Manningham's first occupant. The house was four storeys tall originally, but was reduced to two storeys in 1828 and the stone used to build another wing.

Thomas Merritt's gravestone
photograph: C Buller

The path led us to the old churchyard, which is managed by Cornwall Wildlife Trust. Coming to the churchyard, there is much to see here, starting with 50 gravestones commemorating the airmen and one woman associated with the RAF base at Nancecuke. Further on, in amongst rambling brambles and a few shy primroses, we turned left to follow a sign pointing to the grave of the composer and miner Thomas

Merritt (1863-1908). His boisterous carols are still very popular (*Hark the Glad Sound* and *Hail Sacred Day*), and he also wrote the 1902 Coronation March for Edward V11.

We returned to the grassy path and, turning left, continued to a wooden bench with an ancient Cornish cross behind it. This has a Latin cross on the west face, and on the east a Maltese cross, both pierced. Turning right in front of the cross, we walked on, past gates on our left to the clock tower which is all that remains of the church standing here in Demelza's time.

The ornate Basset family sarcophagus is to the right, behind the tower and worth looking at. We left the churchyard via the ornamental iron gates we had passed on our way to the tower, and turned right to have a look at Illogan Churchtown which marks the original Illogan in Demelza's time. We followed the road as it veered to the right, passing a row of cottages on the left (one called Lynwood) to a junction where we saw an interesting old house with a granite stone porch. A little further on, on the left, is a building now converted into flats but which was originally the old boys' school. In his Will of 1722, Francis Basset left £5 yearly for charity schools to educate the poor, including this one at Illogan.

Retracing our steps, we followed the sign pointing to the village hall and walked back along Churchtown and turned right by the school along Nance Lane, which we followed round to the left, ignoring the sign to a youth hostel. We were now in a country lane with school buildings on our left and fields to the right.

Illogan began to grow with the miners working for the Bassets, and

Illogan church tower

any children receiving financial help from the church, had to go to work from the age of 7 onwards; if they didn't, the money was stopped. We followed the country lane between hedgerows as it went downhill till we saw a large green tennis court ahead of us, which belonged to Aviary Court, parts of which may be 300 years old. This house was once the home of the celebrated mining engineer James Tangye (his brother was grandfather to Cornish authors Nigel and Derek Tangye) and is now a 3-star hotel which has been owned by the same family for over 30 years.

Ignoring the entrance to Illogan Woods (through which Demelza and her siblings no doubt walked to Portreath), we turned left by the tennis court and passed an old pump on a bank, where budding daffodils nodded their heads gently in the breeze, and saw Barnyard, now a holiday cottage complex but was originally Glebe Farm and thought to have been the rectory before Manningham.

From Barnyard we headed up Well Lane and at a T-junction, turned right onto Parsonage Lane, where we saw large green clumps of leaves promising rows of blue and white Agapanthus in the summer, and primrose buds waiting for warmer weather.

The Basset family made their fortune out of mining in this area, with land that included Portreath, with its safe and accessible harbour. Copper was mined from the16th century, while tin mining dominated from the 1800s, reaching a peak in the 1870s. Cornwall was the most important place in the world for mining until the 1840s and the Bassets, their mines and their workers, were central to this industry.

Until the late 1700s Portreath was mainly a fishing village surrounded by farms, but with the advent of mining, it was developed so that tin and copper ore could be shipped to Wales and Welsh coal brought back. So in Demelza's time, the harbour would have been full of bustling industrial activity, with a huge fleet of schooners, brigs and brigantines – Demelza may well have stood by the harbour watching the ships load and unload.

From the late 1800s the harbour became much quieter and Portreath's transformation as a holoday resort began. On the beach you can still see the bathing pools that Lord Bassett had cut into the rocks so that his daughter could safely bathe in the seawater. Now it is a busy holiday resort, but there are still remains of its mining past, when it was at the centre of the world's mining history.

At the top of the hill we found signs saying Mineral Trail, pointing right onto a wide track which was once part of the Portreath Tram Road, but we went straight on, heading for a Public Footpath sign, beside the entrance to a property called Ravenshaw. We went through what was once a metal kissing gate and down a narrow path with laurel trees on the left and a high wooden fence on our right. We were now following the track that the Basset family would have taken in their carriages, and their servants on foot, from the big house at Tehidy, to worship at Illogan Church. The path was quite uneven here and robins and blackbirds sang above us as we walked along. Demelza would have walked along this level path which crosses over other smaller paths and is criss-crossed by myriad tree roots.

The road we were now standing beside is Cot Road and we crossed over, turned left along it and walked the short distance to the entrance to what was once part of the Basset family estate but is now Tehidy Country Park, with more than nine miles of paths and 250 acres of woods (the largest area of woodland in west Cornwall) and lakes with a cafe and picnic area, though dogs are not allowed around the lakes, which ruled us out with MollieDog.

Through some granite gateposts, we came to Eastern Lodge; a thatched building that looked just like a fairytale gingerbread house. On our left the land had all been Tehidy Estate and parkland but is now a golf course. We took the first right to East Lodge car park, but if we had continued straight on and into the woods, following signs to the lakes, we would have got a glimpse of Tehidy Mansion. William Basset obtained the manor of Tehidy in 1150 and the house was built in

Eastern Lodge, Tehidy

1734 with the profits from copper mining. The house was rebuilt in 1861, after the family had made a fortune from the tin mines on their land, and described as the finest modern building in Cornwall.

When Ross and Demelza attend a party there, she notices that, surrounded by moorland and mining, it was pleasantly wooded, with a fine deer park and pretty lake overlooked by the house. It was set in 700 acres – a square Palladian mansion: at each of its corners stood a pavilion or smaller house, one of which was a chapel, another a huge conservatory and the other two housed servants.

The Bassets left Tehidy in 1916 when Arthur Basset had gambled the rest of the family fortune on horses. (In the Poldark novels, Lord Basset shot himself.) The house subsequently became a hospital for sufferers of chest diseases, notably tuberculosis. It remained a hospital until 1983 when the house and surrounding land were acquired by the local authority and the woodland became a country park. In 1995 the rest of the main house, buildings and gardens were sold to the Raven Group, who specialise in converting old buildings and they developed numerous upmarket residential housing units.

At the east car park we kept the parking area on our left while following the path back onto Cot Road. We crossed to a broad track visible through a gate on the other side, beside a sign reading 'The Cornish Way. Mining Trails. Portreath 1.5 miles'. This tram road, along which mules pulled wheeled carts on metal plates, brought mineral ore to the harbour and bringing coal to the mines.

As we walked, the wind turbine in the adjacent field made a huge swishing noise, almost as if it were about to take off, while we could see St Agnes Beacon, on our right, and the white dome of the site of RAF Portreath loomed ahead. The dome protects the radar dish inside from the worst of the elements battering the north coast. RAF Portreath airfield was very active in the Second World War but is now known as Remote Radar Head Portreath because its principal function is to maintain the radar protecting the country's south western approaches.

We continued to the end of the path where it led into a paved area by some large timber holiday chalets. Here we turned right, signposted 'Illogan 1 mile', along a bridleway popular with dog walkers; we were accosted by a very friendly blue-grey greyhound, then greeted by a collection of other dogs – and their owners – as we walked along.

From here there's a wonderful view of the surrounding countryside: behind us the sea off the north coast is visible. Ignoring the farm track to the right, we skirted a hillock with a picnic table on top, and in the distance to the left were silhouettes of abandoned mine engine houses – a reminder of the principal occupation here in Demelza's day. We could also see Illogan church tower and the roofs of the school buildings we passed earlier.

We followed the path round to the left with another field of daffodils on our left and some bee hives. Redruth sprawled ahead of us, in the distance, and also Carn Brea, which was once part of the Basset estate, and its castle, which was used as a hunting lodge by the Basset family but it is now a restaurant. Its 90 foot high granite obelisk was built in 1836 in memory of Francis Basset, Lord de Dunstanville, while on our left we could see Illogan Woods (also owned by the Tehidy estate), which we passed earlier.

At the end of this path we turned right, following a sign reading Mineral Trails towards a farmyard and some converted barns, and then left again, following the Mining Trails sign, past a farm with a collection of mobile homes presumably inhabited by farm workers. We were now on a wide, potholed farm track with tethered kites flying as bird scarers in the fields; a black one looked like a predatory bird, about to pounce. On our left we could see St Agnes Beacon and much nearer, Manningham House on our left through the trees.

At the end of the farm track we saw we'd arrived back at the point where earlier we'd taken the footpath on the right next to the house called Ravenshaw. This time we went straight along Parsonage Lane and followed a green Public Footpath sign down a gravelled path with a tall wooden fence on our right. At the end of this path we turned left into Alexandra Road. This is part of the new road built by the Bassets which led, direct as the crow flies, from the East Lodge of their home at Tehidy, bypassing the town of Redruth, and on to join the coach road to London – which is now the A30.

Walking past a very tuneful blackbird, we passed the first gentle daffodils, a magnolia with shy buds, and came to Alexandra House, one of the oldest houses in Illogan, and continued until we came back to where we'd parked. There are several old, handsome granite houses along here: the one past the pasty shop dates back to the Poldark era, but Illogan continued to grow after the tin mining boom, and there are modern houses on both sides of the road now.

Alexandra House, Illogan

It was fascinating to walk along the paths that Demelza and her family would have walked along, to imagine her father and brothers trudging to and from the mines, maybe attending church on Sundays. Illogan was a parish of extremes in Poldark times. There were the Bassets in their mansion of Tehidy, surrounded by the land and mines that they owned, entertaining lavishly, while the poor of Illogan struggled daily to survive and avoid the workhouse. Many miners died or were badly hurt down the mines, and widows and their children received no compensation.

In *Tehidy and the Bassets – the rise and fall of a great Cornish family*, Michael Tangye quotes a local person: "I used to go to the gate of the lodge watching the widows of miners pass up the drive. They were given an article of their choice – a coat, blanket or a hundredweight of coal. They thought the Bassets were wonderful. They'd forgotten their husbands had died at 30 years of age for their benefit!" The widows took the coal home in wheelbarrows.

A stark reminder of the harshness of life in Poldark times.

GODOLPHIN HOUSE
used as Trenwith in the 1970s Poldark series

Trenwith is one of the main locations in the Poldark books, and anyone who has read the books will know that this house is definitely a major feature.

In the 1970s TV series, Godolphin House was used to film Trenwith, the Poldark family home where Francis and Verity were brought up, and where Aunt Agatha lived with them. Francis inherited the house from his father, Charles, and lived there while married to Elizabeth; after Francis died, Elizabeth stayed on with her son, Geoffrey Charles, and when she married George Warleggan, they lived between Trenwith, Cardew and the Warleggan house in Truro.

When Elizabeth died, George closed the house up, returning just once a year, and the house was left in trust to Geoffrey Charles Poldark, who brought his Spanish bride, Amadora, back there after their marriage. He opened up the almost derelict house and brought it back to life.

In the last episode of the first 1970s TV series, script writers deviated from the books and wrote a scene in which miners went on the rampage and burnt down Trenwith. This was filmed at Godolphin Hall with the permission of the owner, Mr Schofield, who was most concerned that his over-realistic fires might melt the lead of his gutterings and down pipes.

At the beginning of the 2015 Poldark series, Ross arrived at Trenwith on his return from fighting in America. Having made it to Truro by coach, he found no Jud Paynter or horse waiting for him as requested, so he borrowed a lame horse from the innkeeper and made his way home to Nampara, calling in at Trenwith, to see his cousin Francis on the way.

I imagine an exhausted Ross, horse clip clopping up the driveway to Trenwith (Godolphin) on a dark winter's night, the rain lashing and a biting north easterly wind blowing. He saw lights burning inside, rays of candle light illuminating the dark rooms. Expecting a friendly welcome at the house, he knocked on the door – only to find his beloved fiancee Elizabeth betrothed to his cousin, and his world turned upside down....

What you need to know	
Distance	3½ miles approximately
Allow	2½ hours
Suggested Map	OS Explorer 102 Penzance & St Ives
Starting point	Godolphin car park; grid reference SW 599319
Terrain	Steep in parts, can be very muddy
Nearest refreshments	Godolphin cafe (The Piggery) check website for opening times: www.nationaltrust.org.uk/godolphin/ Also Lion & Lamb pub at Ashton
Public transport	Camborne 9 miles; Bus 39 from Helston to Penzance
Of interest	Godolphin House; Cookworthy's quarry; Germoe War Memorial; Castle Pencaire; Preaching Pit, Site of Special Scientific Interest
Facilities	Toilets at Godolphin House

Directions

From Helston take the A394 to Sithney Common, turn right onto the B3302 to Leedstown, turn left and follow the signs to Godolphin. From Hayle take the B3302 to Leedstown, turn right and follow the signs. From the west, B3280 through Goldsithney, turn right at Townshend and follow the signs.

On an overcast afternoon in October, I met Jon and Annie in the main car park near Godolphin House (parking free at time of writing) and headed right up the road towards the house. We turned left following the sign towards the entrance with a field on our left and a copse of beech and sycamore trees on our right. Walking over a wooden bridge, with deciduous woods on either side, we continued towards the elegant Godolphin house which is well worth a look

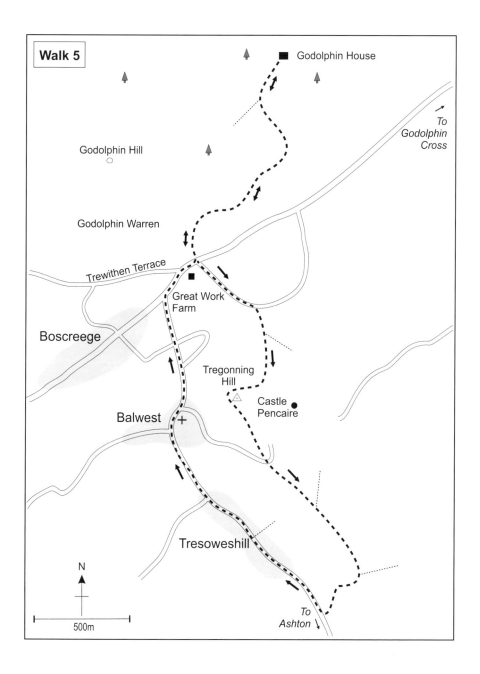

Walk 5

Godolphin House

To Godolphin Cross

Godolphin Hill

Godolphin Warren

Trewithen Terrace

Great Work Farm

Boscreege

Tregonning Hill

Castle Pencaire

Balwest

Tresoweshill

To Ashton

N

500m

60

around. Leaving the house on our left, we went through a gate that says Godolphin Hill.

Here we had to consult the map – I had done this walk many months ago but with Col, and I couldn't remember exactly which way we'd gone. But Jon and Annie helped identify the route, so we walked diagonally roughly south west across the middle of a large, square field "with a small wood ahead of us at the end of the field," called Jon, striding ahead, calling instructions.

Godolphin Hill lay on our right, and Tregonning Hill diagonally ahead to the south as we came to a wooden five barred gate and turned right, crunching our way over the fallen sycamore leaves under our feet. Here we headed up a stony track – possibly a drover's path – and came to a big wooden stile on our left leading to a large field of inquisitive cows with their calves.

Putting Moll on the lead (you never know about cows and their calves), we followed the left hand hedge round the perimeter of this large field, looked at askance by all the cows, with some adorable calves with brown and white faces. We continued round the edge of the field, to a gate at the far end, which we passed through and followed another drover's lane heading uphill towards Tregonning Hill.

At a fork we decided to go left, along a very wiggly, rough little path punctuated by small granite boulders. This path would be extremely muddy after rain, so beware. On either side of us were hawthorn trees, bleak in their winter nudity, and chestnut brown bracken at the end of its life for this year. The path meandered around while we sampled the last of the blackberries which were very good – and late – this year.

Following the line of telegraph poles, we headed uphill, with Jon leading, Moll padding in his footsteps. Coming to where the track meets the road, we took a grassy lane parallel to the road, climbing uphill all the way, with brambles on either side, even the odd bramble flower, plenty of gorse and a few bindweed flowers.

Joining the road we could see, ahead of us, a triangular grassy patch, but before we reached it, we took a left down Granny Polly Lane with a mine engine house on our right. This is a tarmac lane with Great Work Farm on our right, and other houses on our left, and the most incredible hydrangeas sporting opulent autumn blooms of pinky blue, lilac and greeny pink.

On our left we noticed woods behind a house, and a surprising garden on our right, lovingly created from a cleared section of moorland. We got the feeling this would look beautiful in spring as well as summer, with a pine tree hovering protectively over the garden, where someone has placed picnic tables and chairs, added potted plants so that visitors can enjoy the fabulous views in peace and quiet.

We continued along the lane, scrunching sycamore leaves underfoot, with the garden on our right and some stone owls on granite gateposts on our left. Further along, we hit a grassy, boggy lane and took a right fork up onto the moorland. The path here is narrow, winding and steep – "You don't realise how high up we are here," said Jon, as we paused to take a breath, looking out over Mounts Bay to the west in the distance, St Michael's Mount a tiny castle peeping out of the low clouds.

The best time to enjoy Tregonning Hill is in late summer or early autumn, when the purple heather and yellow gorse are at their best. Bilberries, or whortleberries, also grow here in autumn, and it's possible to see the increasingly scarce Lawn Chamomile with its aromatic white summer flowers and finely dissected leaves.

War memorial

Amphibians and insects such as Palmate Newt, the toad, grass snake and adders love the ponds on Tregonning Hill, as do dragonflies and damselflies. We noted kestrels and buzzards, but hen harriers can also be seen here hunting for mice and other creatures.

Coming to a fork with a yellow waymark sign to the left, we opted to take the right hand path, but there are numerous paths leading over Tregonning Hill so it doesn't matter too much which one you take, though most are strewn with granite boulders, so watch your step.

Climbing ever higher, a monument loomed up on our right – Jon got there first and claimed first seat on the wooden bench in front of the memorial which was built of stone from the original ramparts of Castle Pencaire. This was reputedly the site of an abode of giants, with two ramparts and ditches with east and west entrances. There is evidence of hut circles within the site, though these have been much disturbed by mining and prospecting, so it's difficult to see how they would have been originally.

Hill forts were more likely used for trade, serving as a gathering point for community ceremonies, rather than for defence: the impressive ditches are now thought to be a symbol of power and status. On the ridge to the south of Castle Pencaire is a Bronze Age barrow where a Roman coin hoard was discovered, suggesting activity in the area both before and after the period during which the hillfort would have been at its height. The Celts were excellent farmers and we could still see field patterns dating back to this time on the eastern slopes of the hill.

From the war memorial – 637 feet above sea level – we enjoyed the most incredible views of the Lizard, to our left, sweeping round to Mounts Bay in the west ahead of us, and St Ives to our right. To the north is Leeds Shaft engine house of Great Work Mine nestling at the base of Godolphin Hill, covered in bracken. All around are acres and acres of fields, interrupted by the odd farm or house – the views of both coasts can't have changed much for hundreds of years.

From the memorial it's worth taking a short diversion to the trig point, which has a metal plaque on top giving a clear indication of what you can see from here, in great detail. Below us we could see Bal West and the Methodist Chapel, from where there are numerous footpaths leading up to the hill.

TREGONNING HILL TRIG POINT
OS. BM S1722
HEIGHT 194 METRES
LAT. 05.21.5 W LONG. 50.07.3 N
GRID REF. SW 5992 3005

Tegonning Hill trig point

Tregonning Hill forms a ridge running south-eastwards, so we followed the path along the ridge which showed signs of recent work – steps had been dug out. Heading south down a stony track, we found a Preaching Pit (a smaller version of Gwennap Pit, near Redruth) where Ashton Methodists have long congregated on Whit Sundays, and nowadays Christians of many denominations meet annually for ecumenical services. In the fields to the left was Wheal Bunny, though there are no signs of the mine today, bar an old stone kiln which is a remnant from the Tregonning Brick & Clay Works, where building and fire bricks were made.

In 1871, William Argall, an experienced mine captain from Breage, realised there was no great future or fortune to be made from exporting china clay only, so he proposed switching to brickmaking. With financial backing from two local iron founders, William Harvey of Hayle and John Toy of Helston, kilns and drying sheds were built on the northern slopes of Tregonning Hill at Wheal Bunny.

They made two kinds of bricks: firebricks for hearths and building bricks, and each brick was incised 'Tregonning Hill'. The company did well, expanding to take over the Tresowes and Wheal Grey setts, and building more kilns and brickmaking works near Tresowes Green, so that by 1890, William Argall and Company controlled the whole area.

A large source of clay had also been found in the Leeds pit, and if you look over the hill west towards Germoe, the pits still remain, though they are now filled with water and overgrown with gorse. It's also possible to see the remains of the brick kilns.

In 1893, William Argall's retirement present was an Asiatic Pheasant dinner service, especially emblazoned with Argall's monogram *WA* surrounded by Tregonning Hill. Some of the remaining pieces can be seen at Helston Folk Museum.

Further on from the Preaching Pit was a large quarry which is where china clay was first extracted by William Cookworthy (1705-80), a Quaker chemist from Plymouth, in the middle of the 18th century. In 1746 Captain Nancarrow from Great Work Mine invited Cookworthy to stay with him at Godolphin. While visiting the mine, Cookworthy saw the men were repairing the furnaces with clay found on the slopes of Tregonning Hill.

The chemist took samples back to his laboratory and found that when either petunse (aluminium and potassium silicate) + china stone, or kaolin (aluminium silicate) + china clay were fired together to a great heat, both combinations produced porcelain.

As a result, he leased various clay pits on Tregonning Hill, evidence of which can still be seen today. Clay was exported from Porthleven to Cookworthy's factory in Plymouth, but the clay contains dark specks of mica so wasn't of the best quality. Two years later, purer clay was found at St. Austell, so the Tregonning clay industry declined but lasted until the early years of the 20th century. China clay enabled the production of English porcelain, exported internationally to over 100 countries. Today its use is widespread in the manufacture of paper, paints, rubber and plastic.

Cookworthy commemorative plaque

Continuing south east along the ridge, we eventually came to a big stone stile and huge granite blocks on the far side of a five barred gate which led into a farmyard on our right. We walked through the farmyard, with dogs barking, and were greeted by the most wonderful views down to Breage on our left, Porthleven, where Jon and Annie were staying, Breage, and Loe Bar beyond that, with the wide sweep of Mounts Bay beyond. This farmhouse is Tregonning House, and we walked down the tarmac drive enjoying the rich landscape before us. A seat was carefully positioned on our left, for those wishing to enjoy these dramatic views at leisure.

Reaching the bottom of the drive we came to a minor road and turned right by a Germoe Parish noticeboard containing information about Tregonning

Hill. Strolling along, we picked the last blackberries, noted blackberry flowers and campion, and passed Tremorvu campsite on the left.

Set back from the road we found an adit on our right draining water from the china clay workings on the side of Tregonning Hill. These workings post date 1746, the year when Cookworthy first realised that the clay extracted from the local moor stone was in fact china clay. Nowadays the water is no longer used for industrial purposes.

Ignoring signs to Tresowes Green on our left, we carried on along the road, coming to Balwest and Germoe on the left. There are numerous paths along here on the right which would doubtless take you back to Tregonning Hill, but we continued along the road past Balwest methodist church and a little cemetery on the left.

Passing a kitten rescue stall (we'd bought books there last time, but there were plants and apples on display, both of which we had in abundance), we continued along the road passing a sign to Mount Whistle, coming to a sign to Godolphin Cross and another noticeboard.

Returning to Granny Polly Lane, we found the grassy path parallel to the main road and headed back towards Godolphin, the way we came. The bracken strewn path revealed several violets – unusual for this time of year, and the trees were shedding the last of their leaves, revealing stark winter skeletons against a grey, Cornish slate sky.

MollieDog had rolled in something quite disgusting, but luckily the fields were full of long, wet grass, which washed her off enough to avoid a stinky car journey back.

We'd hoped to have a cup of tea at the cafe at Godolphin but sadly we were too late, so check opening times of the cafe before walking. Take the time to have a look around the elegant Doric colonnaded house of Godolphin, its rambling gardens, and reflect, as we did, on the many events that this house – as Trenwith – would have witnessed. The birth of Francis and Verity Poldark. The death of Charles, their father; the marriage of Elizabeth to Francis, and Ross's sense of betrayal that did nothing to lessen his feelings for her. Verity's absconding to marry Andrew Blamey; the birth of Geoffrey Charles and later, the death of Aunt Agatha. When Francis died, Elizabeth stayed on here with her son, before marrying George Warleggan.

Returning to the car park in that late afternoon light that the Cornish call 'dimpsy', I swear I could see Francis cantering down the drive, jumping off his horse, throwing his reins to an ostler and hurrying into the house to see his wife and son. Much later, Clowance Poldark was trespassing at Trenwith and surprised George Warleggan on an impromptu visit, giving him a bunch of foxgloves. After Elizabeth's death, the poor house fell into disrepair for many years, abandoned by its family, before Geoffrey Charles Poldark finally returned with his Spanish wife and the house became a home again.

In the eerie half light, I like to think of the candles being lit, of the clank of pots and pans in the kitchen as an evening meal was prepared. Of love and gentle laughter coming from its rooms as the Poldark family was reinstated, and Trenwith came into its own once more.

LEVANT AND CROWN ENGINE HOUSES AT BOTALLACK

The mining heart of Poldark

Levant and Botallack are two of the most iconic mines in Cornwall, embodying the very spirit of the era when Cornish mining was at its most successful, and when you're here, you will see why. Levant has the oldest beam engine in Cornwall which has been lovingly restored by the National Trust and the Trevithick Society (named after Richard Trevithick, who invented a steam locomotive 12 years before George Stephenson). The Crowns Engine Houses at Botallack are possibly the most photographed mines in Cornwall, perched

Arsenic Labyrinth at Botallack mine

on the very edge of magnificent cliffs, a true testament to the Cornish search for tin and copper.

In the 2015 Poldark TV series, Owles and Crowns Engine Houses double up as Wheal Leisure, the family mine Ross tries to resurrect in order to bring prosperity back to the local area, while Levant Mine was used as Tressiders Rolling Mill, where copper extracted from the mine is processed.

Both Levant and Botallack mines are now part of the Cornish Mining World Heritage Site. This area is peppered with mine workings, so please be careful where you walk, in particular if you have young children or dogs.

In the first part of the 18th century the Poldarks profited from the great Grambler mine, and the smaller Wheal Leisure and Wheal Grace mines. Cornwall was famous for its tin, particularly in the west of the county, with many people dependent on the mines for their livelihoods.

When Ross was young, Wheal Leisure had been worked for surface tin only, but Ross knew that there were definite signs of copper, which is found underground so miners have to dig tunnels and sink shafts. When Wheal Leisure was opened, ironstone was found at once, being a good indicator of copper, but explosives were needed to get at it, which was expensive.

As George Lipscomb wrote, in *A Journey into Cornwall* 1799, "The Miners are a race distinct from the common class of British subjects: they are governed by laws and customs almost exclusively their own; and wild as their native rocks, and rugged as the hordes of Africa they are separated from."

To try and break the Warleggan's stranglehold on copper prices in Cornwall, Ross and other investors secretly started their own smelting company, the Carnmore Copper Company. This was based on the real Cornish Metal Company, established in 1784 to compete against South Wales and Bristol companies. Between 1784 and 1792, the Cornish Metal Company bought all the copper ore raised, converted it to copper and tried to market it, but with little success.

The Carnmore Copper Company in Poldark was dissolved after a year because other smelting companies, backed by the Warleggans, priced them out of the market and starved them of the copper ore they needed.

In the 1770s and 1780s the price of tin fell because of a national economic depression, increased competition from Welsh mines, and the smelting companies keeping their prices artificially low (as the Warleggans did) to maximise profits. This caused widespread resentment, particularly among miners who were also affected by low copper prices. As a result Wheal Leisure was forced to close, though Ross reopened it at a later date.

What you need to know	
Distance	3 miles approximately
Allow	2 hours
Suggested Map	OS Landranger 203 Land's End & Isles of Scilly, St Ives & Lizard Point
Starting point	Botallack car park; grid reference SW 365332
Terrain	Rough: beware of mine workings
Nearest refreshments	Nearest in Pendeen or St Just: the Bookshop Cafe and Dog and Rabbit in St Just both recommended
Public transport	Regular buses between Penzance and Pendeen – ring 08712002233 or www.travelinesw.com
Of interest	Crown Engine Houses at Botallack and Levant Mines; the Count House
Facilities	Nearest toilets in Pendeen or St Just Stay in a gypsy caravan www.gypsycaravanbandb.co.uk

Directions

From St Just, Mr B, MollieDog and I took the B3306 towards St Ives and turned first left at Botallack, then followed the signs to the free car park. We left the van and walked around the mine workings lit by a frail winter sun, as I imagined how this must have been in Poldark times; the bal-maidens working above ground, sorting the tin with their children, while their husbands laboured in the stifling tunnels underground.

At the first shaft, immediately left you will see stone walls that mark the remains of the miners' changing house, or 'dry'. Return to the path and continue to the triangulation pillar, then the ruined chimney stack; on the left

Allens Shaft headgear and old calciner chimney from Botallack mine

of this path are the remains of Botallack's 19th-century copper-dressing floors. Here women and children worked to break and separate the valuable copper ores from the waste rock.

Ross fought to get conditions improved not only for the miners and women working at the mines, but also for the children, thus earning himself a reputation as something of a radical thinker, which was not approved of by the gentry.

Returning to the main track, we turned right and followed the path for about 70m and at the Coast Path marker stone, followed the path southwards (marked St Just 1½ miles). This took us past the 1906 tin-dressing floors and arsenic works: arsenic was a lucrative by-product of tin ore. Above the path are the remains of a square building with a distinctive archway in buff-coloured brickwork: this was a Brunton calciner, and was the starting point for the extraction of arsenic from Botallack ores during the 1906-1914 re-working.

Walking among the remains of the mines here, you can almost hear the clanking of the engines, the hiss of the steam, the chatter of the women at

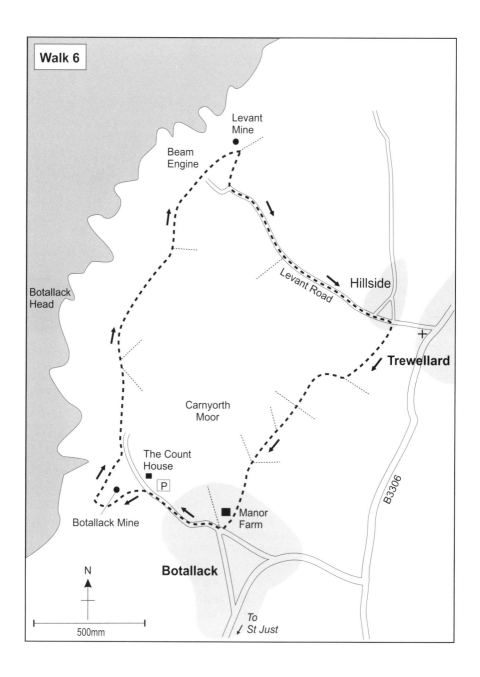

Walk 6

Levant Mine

Beam Engine

Botallack Head

Levant Road

Hillside

Trewellard

Carnyorth Moor

The Count House

P

Botallack Mine

Manor Farm

Botallack

B3306

N

500mm

To
St Just

Arsenic flues at Botallack

work outside, the mumblings of the men as they emerged from a long shift underground. Here you can feel the mining history all around you, and appreciate how much a part of Cornwall, and Poldark, it truly is.

As we followed the coastal footpath, a lifeboat set forth on this still afternoon, the familiar blue and orange boat ploughing through the water, while the waves were a distant hush as they crashed against the rocks. There is evidence of mining activity all around us, and the path is uneven with rocks and granite boulders strewn among the gorse and heather, so be careful.

On the horizon we could see the outline of the Isles of Scilly, and as we walked round Botallack Head a crow gave its crackly cry above us. Out to sea, a trawler chugged its way through the grey-green flat seas, while ahead of us the stark white column of Pendeen Watch lighthouse gleamed in the winter sunshine. Standing on Botallack Head we looked down to Natural Arch, a dramatic formation of black rock, with waves breaking around and through it.

If you're lucky you may see choughs flying overhead – they are easily distinguished from other members of the crow family by their red bills and legs and their distinctive 'cheeow' call. The chough became extinct in England when the last bird died in the 1970s, but reintroduction of grazing to coastal grasslands and heaths has improved the short, open vegetation that they rely on for feeding. A breeding pair of choughs was brought back to Lizard Point in 2002 and from then on there has been a slow recovery of the Cornish chough population.

A couple of ponies rode past making me think of Ross and mine Captain Henshaw riding towards the mine. The workers often walked miles in order to work a twelve hour day, six days a week. Demelza might have walked over these cliff paths to arrive with a basket of saffron buns for the miners, Garrick lolloping along beside her.

In the near distance, Levant mine loomed up out of the heather, like a small mining village. Known as 'the mine beneath the sea', the Levant mine workings extend over a mile out under the sea bed at a depth of over 300 fathoms. In 1820, the Levant Mining Company was formed to mine copper and tin, with a capital of £400, though Levant Mine first appeared on a map in 1748. By 1836, 320 men, 44 women and 186 children were employed on the site. In addition

Levant mine

Crowns Engine House

to copper and tin, long flues were built to collect arsenic as a fine white dust, and young boys were sent in, covered in a protective layer of clay, to scrape the arsenic from the flue walls. The arsenic was used in pesticides, glass making, dyes for carpets, paints and wallpaper.

In the first twenty years of production, Levant made £170,000 from mining copper. New technology was introduced to streamline production, and in 1857 the now infamous man-engine was installed. This engine carried men many fathoms up and down the mine, to and from work each day. But in 1919, a link between the rod and the man-engine snapped, killing 31 men. From then on, Levant declined until the mine closed in 1930.

Reaching Levant mine car park (free to National Trust members), the man-engine shaft and the ruin of the engine house are just up the slope. We headed up the road, which winds gradually uphill past a farm on the right until we came to a gypsy caravan. As we stood admiring it, the owner came out and gave us a guided tour of the caravan which is being lovingly restored and is available for B&B – details in information box on page 70. You can even take the dog – a romantic spot for an intimate get away!

Continuing along the road, we passed the remains of Higher Bal mine – look at the massive walls, about 10 feet thick – and continued up this road until we reached Hillside, a small hamlet with a large (deserted) granite farmhouse on the right and a bench in front of it. We followed a muddy farm track, alongside the house, past a stable with a pretty grey pony inside, and continued on this track past a sharp bend, ignoring the first waymark sign on the left, until we came to a yellow waymark sign over a granite stile in the hedge on the left, next door to a large wooden five barred gate. From here, we headed for the farm in the distance, following a succession of stiles over fields, as follows.

Having climbed over the first stile, this led across a field to another stile, where we dropped down into a field with an electric fence marking the footpath with a tall hedge on the right. This led to a granite stile into another field, and after a few yards we climbed over a stile in a hedge on the right into the next field. There we found a waymark sign on the right by a cluster of gorse bushes, with a smattering of brilliant yellow flowers.

Crossing the field diagonally, we came to a granite stile with waymark signs on the top, pointing to left and right – we took the left hand path, worn by footmarks in the grass, and crossed another field and stile, heading for the farm ahead. Rejoicing in the first primroses, we climbed over more stiles which brought us into a muddy field with cattle in. Heading for the far right hand side of this field to find another stile, we climbed over this to arrive at a farm track where we turned left.

We passed Manor Farm on our right and continued along the path until we came to Botallack Manor where we turned right, back along the road we'd driven in on. "This is just how I imagined Nampara to be," I said to Mr B – then later found out that this house had been used to portray Nampara in the second original TV series in the 1970s.

Further on, we came to a large property with a conservatory: this was the old Count House of the mine and was built around 1861 as the residence and offices for the Captain and staff of the Botallack Mine. This was where the mine accounts were done, and where mine workers would come, once a month, to get their wages. When Cornish mining was at its most successful, lavish dinners would take place at the count houses, when shareholders gathered to examine the mine accounts. More recently it has been a venue for folk concerts.

Nowadays you can stay next door, at Count House Cottage: a good place to explore the coastal footpath, but we were staying at Penzance, so we continued back along the road until we reached the car park, where we returned to St Just for a very welcome coffee in the Dog and Rabbit cafe (where they do welcome dogs!) – a perfect end to a very beautiful walk, full of mining heritage and redolent of Poldark with every step.

In the Poldark series, Winston Graham takes us on a journey that involves love and loss, heartbreak and great joy. But the mining aspect does not merely provide a backdrop: the mines and their workers underpin the entire story. Without it, the Poldarks would not have existed.

PORTHGWARRA AND PORTHCURNO

Scene of the longed for pilchard catch

and a daring escape

Porthgwarra cove is used for the many fishing scenes in the 2015 TV series of Poldark, including the landing of a pilchard catch, which was so vital not only to the local economy but to the Cornish diet. During the Poldark series, villagers are often seen on the clifftops looking out for pilchards. When a 'huer' spotted the longed for pilchard shoals, which arrive in late summer, he would call, "Heva! Heva!", and the locals would immediately stop work and rush to bring in the haul.

Porthgwarra beach

The fish would be brought ashore then gutted and stacked in layers of salt, where they could be stored for weeks, to feed the villagers, or exported abroad. The oil was also used for lighting lamps and some gave it to their children to keep them strong and healthy.

Later in the series Ross helps Mark Daniels avoid arrest for the murder of his wife, by lending him his dinghy so he can escape from Porthgwarra, which doubles as Nampara Cove.

The small village of Porthcurno is famous worldwide because of its international submarine communications cable station. In the late 19th century, early submarine telegraph cables from here formed part of a link from UK to India, which was then a British colony. In 1872 the Eastern Telegraph Company was formed to operate the cables from an office in Porthcurno valley. The company expanded in the 19th and 20th centuries to merge with Marconi's Wireless Telegraph Company in 1928 and form Imperial & International Communications Ltd which became Cable and Wireless Limited in 1934.

Between the wars, Porthcurno cable office operated up to 14 cables, becoming the largest submarine cable office in the world, able to receive and transmit up to two million words a day. The cable office closed in 1970, exactly 100 years after the first cable was landed, but the award winning Porthcurno Telegraph Museum has featured in many educational programmes on the BBC.

Once a thriving fishing cove, Porthgwarra sits quietly at the heart of St Aubyn Estates, owned by Lord St Levan. The peaceful valley surrounding the cove is full of wild flowers and is a popular place for spotting rare and migrant birds. If you're lucky you may spot puffins and hoopoes, and many other birds that are blown off course from their migration routes.

According to locals, Porthgwarra was once called 'Sweethearts Cove' because two young lovers, named Nancy and William, met in secret at Porthgwarra before William went to sea. Time passed and he did not return and Nancy grew pale and thin with worry. Often she would wait on the beach until one day, a sailor appeared from the sea, put his arms around her, and they both disappeared into the waves. Soon came the news that William's ship had been wrecked off Porthgwarra and all the crew drowned. So while the couple may not have found each other in this life, they did so in the next.

What you need to know	
Distance	3 miles
Allow	2½ hours to include sandwiches
Suggested Map	OS Explorer 102 Land's End
Starting point	Porthcurno car park; grid reference SW 3842225
Terrain	Some steep hills
Nearest refreshments	Cafe at Porthcurno Telegraph Museum, Minack theatre and seasonal cafe at Porthgwarra. Toilets at Porthcurno. Cable Station Inn open daily from 12 noon
Public transport	1A bus from Penzance to Land's End. Nearest railway station Penzance
Of interest	Porthcurno Cove and Telegraph Museum; St Levan Church; Minack Theatre built out of the cliffs by Rowena Cade see website for programme: www.minack.com
Facilities	Public toilets at Porthcurno and Porthgwarra Parking £4.60 for up to 4 hours at time of walking but parking free from 1st November - 14th March. Dog ban Easter to end September. Porthcurno Museum car park free but you will have to pay to enter the museum though not the cafe

Directions

One sunny Thursday, I set forth from Penzance on the A30 with Deb, Richard and MollieDog, following the signs to Land's End. It was an inauspicious start, as Deb had a dodgy hip that needed replacing imminently, and I'd not long ago twisted my ankle. Rich wasn't admitting to anything dodgy, so we headed off with optimism and painkillers, reflecting that this could possibly be a very short walk.

Beyond Drift, we turned left at Catchall on the B3282 and turned left again at Trethewey to Porthcurno, where we passed the Telegraph Museum and parked in the car park with public toilets which won the Best Loos of 2006. Coming out, we turned right back up the hill, past the Cable Station Inn (open all day) and, several hundred yards later, just before Sea View House, we turned left and walked along a tarmac track with grass down the middle and fields either side, while we looked down on the Telegraph Museum and, seawards, Treryn Dinas fort and the distinctive rocky outcrop of Logan Rock.

The footpath took us past several cottages on our left and through a metal gate we continued along the track till we came to a second metal gate and the remains of a barn on our left and more cottages, we followed the path round to the left to a house called Treveth, near a sign saying 'Dogs to be kept on a lead at all times'. From here we turned right through a metal kissing gate and could just see the steeple of St Levan church peeping over the brow of the hill.

Passing a very ancient granite cross on our right – so old the cross was hardly visible – we walked down a grassy track with fields on either side, through a wooden gate and over a granite stile, into the sheltered churchyard. It was incredibly quiet here: just the sound of birds singing above us. and a stream running down below to our right.

Here in the churchyard we found a massive granite stone which is split neatly in two. According to local folklore, it is where St Levan rested when he was tired of fishing. It was also said:

> *When with panniers astride*
> *A pack horse can ride*
> *Through St Levan's Stone*
> *The world will be done.*

St Levan was named after his great-uncle St Soloman, was reputedly born in the 6th century, and built a chapel on the site of the present church above St Levan some 1500 years ago. The church was rebuilt in the 12th century, extended in the 15th century, and while Deb read us a quick lesson, I saw that the pulpit was built in 1752. The wood carving on the end of the pews and rood screens is well worth admiring, with carvings of a jester in full traditional costume; a pilgrim (possibly St James); a shepherd with crook and two fish on one hook, recalling the legend of St Levan.

Apparently no one has ever been christened Joanna in this church, because in the seventh century, when St Levan was going fishing on a Sunday, he was rebuked for doing so by someone he called Foolish Joanna. They argued until he stormed off, saying that if anyone else was christened with her name, they would be an even bigger fool than she was. After that, any parent wishing to christen their daughter Joanna had to go to St Buryan or Sennen church.

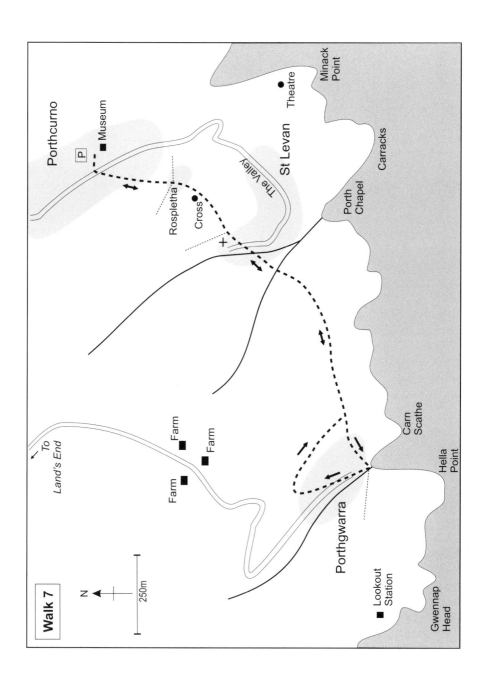

Walk 7

N

250m

To Land's End

Porthcurno

Museum

P

Rospletha

Cross

The Valley

St Levan

Theatre

Minack Point

Carracks

Porth Chapel

Farm

Farm

Farm

Carn Scathe

Hella Point

Porthgwarra

Lookout Station

Gwennap Head

St Levan church

The coastline here is wild and the waters extremely treacherous: a fact borne out by the graves in the churchyard. Near the church tower is the communal grave of 23 men who were lost when the *Khyber* went aground on March 15th, 1905. On the south-west side of the churchyard is the grave of Captain Richard Wetheral of Scilly, who was lost in the brig *Aurora* off Land's End on December 18th, 1811. According to legend, a ghostly ship's bell strikes the watches in his grave and those who hear it are doomed to die within a year.

Perhaps fortunately, we were unaware of these disasters, and wandered among lichen covered stones in the sunshine and admired the sundial over the main entrance before following the path out over the road and a public footpath sign on the right to 'Porthgwarra 1 mile'. While a robin chirped cheerily above us, we followed a rough track by the side of a house with a stream bubbling on our right. We continued down a track over a granite footbridge, up through moorland along a path with toasty bracken on our right and hawthorn thickets on our left.

Coming to a junction we turned right and continued uphill, and at the end of this narrow lane we came to what looked like a large field and turned right again, which led us to the coastal footpath with hawthorn bushes on either side. Three runners passed us, in brightly coloured lycra, and headed off at a fast pace towards Porthgwarra. The cliffs along here have a sculptured beauty, even where it has eroded, leaving boulders like a giant's discarded toys. The sea looked still but swollen today: like stiff cake mixture, or a rumpled bed.

The coastal footpath can be muddy here, with sloe bushes on our left and brambles on our right and, ignoring a footpath to the left, we continued on with the sea pounding as we neared Porthgwarra. Gwennap Head Lookout Station rose up in front of us, with its navigational aids of red and black cones, like miniature rockets. Gwennap Head is the most southerly point of the Land's End peninsula, also known as 'the Fisherman's Land's End'.

The next part of the path was steep, and strewn with large granite boulders: not good for Deb's hip or my dodgy ankle, but with amazing views down over the rugged cliffs at Rockestal (grid reference 374218) and a boulder balanced at an incredible angle on the edge of the cliffs. At a junction, we clambered up

Boulder on cliffs

a flight of wooden steps on our right which led us up a narrow winding path inland through moorland with a few late pink campion showing their faces, and a burst of sweet smelling honeysuckle.

At a tarmac track, just as the sun came out, we turned right opposite what looked like a tiny old school but is now a beautifully restored house, continued uphill and turned left onto the road signposted to Porthgwarra, and continued down this narrow winding road which finally led us to Porthgwarra Cove.

This is reached by a tunnel in the rock at the bottom of the slipway dug out by miners from St Just and used by farmers to carry seaweed to use as fertiliser on their land. There is another tunnel nearer the sea which was used by fishermen so that they could store their catch in tidal 'hulleys' which had wooden floors and top covers with trapdoors. These were used to store the shellfish before taking the catch to market once or twice a week, though they fell into disuse some 20 years ago. The rope on the beach is used to steady boats when landing.

Porthgwarra cove and slipway are privately owned by the St Aubyn estate, but the public are welcome to enjoy them as long as they do so quietly and respectfully. I have yet to come here in summer, but the

Entrance to the beach

Arch at Porthgwarra

swimming looks ideal as long as you don't venture out beyond the headland, where there are strong and dangerous currents.

Porthgwarra Cove Cafe is open in spring and summer serving a limited menu, with a grassy area with picnic tables behind it. We walked down to the cove, which you can do either via a steep slipway or through the tunnel in the rock. Reaching the cove, huge granite rocks towered above us, with surfaces like compressed hay bales, as we sat on a rock in the sunshine, enjoying our sandwiches, fed crisps to Moll and wondered what Porthgwarra had been like as a busy fishing cove. Now just one boat regularly works crab pots from here.

In the 2015 Poldark TV series, the landing of the all-important pilchard catch was filmed at Porthgwarra at night. When the long awaited pilchard shoals came into sight, everyone from Sawle was waiting, either in boats or on the beach. It was deathly quiet, while the seine net was hauled in, and the fishermen could calculate whether it was a good catch or not. Suddenly the waters began to boil and bubble with silver fish, as big a catch as anyone could remember. People shouted in excitement while they filled flat bottomed boats with the fish as fast as they could.

Porthgwarra slip

On the beach, pilchards were shovelled into wheelbarrows and hauled up to the salting cellars, and meanwhile, on and on came the waterfall of the jumping silver fish that would feed the inhabitants of Sawle: the fishermen, the miners and their families, for weeks to come.

This tiny cove was deserted the day we were there, but I could imagine it at night, seething and boiling with the sparkling fish, the delighted cries from the men and women desperate for the free food that would transform their lives for a few short weeks. How lucky I am, I thought, as we walked back up the slipway, not to live in such poverty.

The incident where Ross helped Mark Daniel escape took place at night, and was another example of Ross's eagerness to take part in adventure as a way of helping his friends.

Mark Daniel married Keren, an actress from a travelling theatre company, who soon became bored with life as a miner's wife: Mark worked nights and had no conversation with her anyway. She lured Dr Enys into having an affair – he tried hard to refuse her, being a good man who didn't want to break up a marriage, but she was relentless and wouldn't stop until she got what she wanted, relishing the illicit relationship.

When Mark realised what was going on, he returned from night shift early and confronted Keren, who'd just returned from Dr Enys's bed. She denied any wrong doing, then defied him. Anguished and outraged, they fought, and, not realising his own strength, Mark accidentally broke her neck.

Horrified at what he had done, Mark went into hiding. Realising he would be arrested for murder, Ross agreed to help him escape by lending him his dinghy so he could escape from Nampara Cove and sail over to France. It was an incredibly dangerous ordeal: it was a dark and windy night, and soldiers were stationed all over the cliffs. However, Ross and Mark sneaked out at night, managed to get Mark into the dinghy and out to sea, with the soldiers firing at them.

Ross ran home, dodging soldiers and gunfire, and pretended he'd been in bed, although Captain McNeil knew what he'd done even though he had no proof. Ross stood up for what he believed was right in defying bad laws: McNeil gave him a warning, and warned Ross not to break the law again. But Ross had got away with it.

Porthcurno beach

Leaving the cove we turned right along the coastal footpath, signposted Minack 1¼ miles, with tamarisk trees on either side, past a house called Polventon. We turned right up more granite steps where a lone, dessicated foxglove loomed up among pitty blackberries. Further on, we came to the wooden steps that we'd climbed up on our way here, on the left. Ignoring these, we continued straight on, over more granite boulders. Look out for the wonderfully red-brown lichen growing over these granite slabs – lichen is a sign of the purest air, as it will only grow where the sulphur element in the air is negligible.

Coming to a junction with a path going off to the right, towards the coast, we continued slightly inland, back the way we'd come, to St Levan Church and back to Porthcurno. At Treveth, we were greeted by a very bouncy young collie with the sign of St Piran on his chest, who was very keen to play with Moll.

Reaching Porthcurno beach, famous for its almost white sand made of crushed sea shells, to the east we could see Logan Rock, while to the south west was the famous Minack Open Air Theatre, built by Rowena Cade in 1931.

I have fond memories of a moonlit performance of Romeo and Juliet there many years ago.

After this walk, I have happy memories of a sun kissed autumn day, and a magical walk with very special friends. I will also link it with Mark's escape in Ross's dinghy; of the long awaited pilchard haul. A secret little cove with many Poldark secrets of its own.

I would love to go at night, to walk in Ross's footsteps, maybe take a dinghy out as Ross took Demelza, and watch the moon playing on the inky waters. Who knows what other secrets this cove holds?

WALK EIGHT
PORTHCOTHAN
Nampara Cove

Porthcothan was used in the 2015 Poldark TV series as the location for Nampara Cove, just below Ross Poldark's house. It's here that Ross takes his morning swim as Demelza – who was then his kitchen maid – spies on him. It is to the cove that he comes to unwind, to forget about the pressures in his life – the woman he loves now married to his cousin; his father dead and the house and land in ruins; the quandary over the mine and the economic depression.

Porthcothan

When we first meet Demelza, she is dressed in rags as a boy and fighting in the street to protect her beloved dog, Garrick. Ross rescues her and takes her home to Nampara to work as his kitchen maid. Unlike the idle Paynters, she soon proves her worth and becomes indispensible.

Demelza's love for Ross grows, but she knows it is hopeless. She is aware of his love for Elizabeth – and anyway, why should he so much as look at a poor, uneducated miner's daughter? She is well aware of the problems in his life and accepts that he would never consider her as a partner. But she knows she loves him and the scene where she watches him swim shows us how she feels.

Later, the cove is where Demelza goes when heavily pregnant with Jeremy. Tired of feeling heavy and waiting for the baby to arrive, she sneaks off and takes herself fishing in the rowing boat they keep at Nampara Cove, but drifts out too far. Fighting contractions, she rows herself to the shore, and stumbles up the beach, finally makes it back to Nampara.

What you need to know	
Distance	3 miles
Allow	1¾ hours
Suggested Map	OS Explorer 106 Newquay and Padstow
Starting point	Porthcothan car park; grid reference SW 858719
Terrain	Few steep hills, relatively easy
Nearest refreshments	Porthcothan village stores and Treyarnon Bay cafe in summer only
Public transport	Bus route 56 – for further information ring 08712002233. Newquay railway station is 7 miles away
Of interest	Porthcothan beach, Treynarnon Bay; Youth Hostel at Treyarnon Bay
Facilities	Public toilets at Porthcothan and Treynarnon Bay, summer shops at both beaches

Both beaches are dog friendly year round and there is lifeguard cover from May 22nd to September 30th.

Directions

There were no such encumbrances, thankfully, when Fiona and I set off one December morning. From Newquay we took the B3276 and followed this coast road along Trevarrian Hill, passing through Trevarrian and Trenance before arriving at the small hamlet of Porthcothan. The car park is on the right – this was free at the time of walking, as there are no charges between the end of October and the end of March, but check for charges in the summer season.

From here we crossed the road and walked onto the beach; a north west-facing cove backed by grassy dunes. At low tide, the beach links up with small coves to the north and south and at high tide the cliffs shelter the beach from swell and winds. There are numerous rock pools to poke around in, reminding me of blissful hours as a child spent in this way. This cove is not usually used by surfers, who frequent Constantine Bay for its consistently good surf: Porthcothan is for paddlers, swimmers and sunbathers.

We explored the beach at half tide, along with numerous other dog walkers, then walked alongside the stream, which was too deep to cross, until we came to a small bridge by the road, and crossed this to find the coastal footpath heading north, towards Treyarnon Bay.

Climbing uphill we passed a group of possible Ramblers, all kitted out with walking boots and sticks, peeling off outer layers as despite the stiff wind, it was very warm. At the next junction, because of the wind and because I was nervous about Moll being too close to the cliff edge, we took a path leading away from the cliffs. A lone man walking the outer path paused at the headland to take photographs, but I wasn't going to argue with these near gale force winds – I didn't want to lose Moll or myself.

The headland and cliffs to the north of Porthcothan are owned by the National Trust which protects the wildlife. As we walked, we enjoyed stunning views towards Dinas Head, then Trevose Head and the lighthouse, and as we walked around the headland, we could see several of the Trescore Islands, then Will's Rock, and further on, inlets with delightful names – Fox Cove, Warren Cove and Pepper Cove.

We followed the coastal footpath which, in various places, has been diverted, no doubt due to coastal erosion. We found a beautiful old wall as a fine example of Cornish hedging, with banks of tufty grass on top, and pinks poking their winter faces out. Tamarisk trees grew in abundance on top of

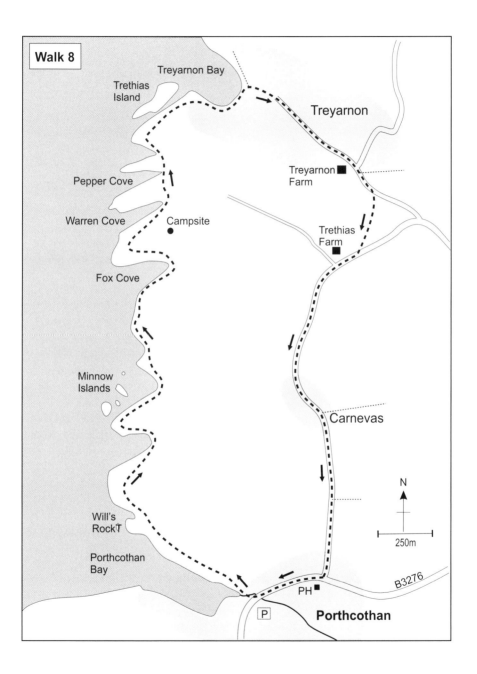

Walk 8

Treyarnon Bay

Trethias Island

Treyarnon

Pepper Cove

Treyarnon Farm ■

Warren Cove   Campsite ●

Trethias Farm ■

Fox Cove

Minnow Islands

Carnevas

N

Will's Rock⊤

250m

Porthcothan Bay

B3276

PH ■

P

Porthcothan

93

the hedge, giving it the air of a windswept professor.

Buffeted by the wind, we went through a few kissing gates, while the waves below were tossed around as if an angry giant had thrown huge rocks into the water. These rocks are the Minnows Islands (grid reference SW854327).

Cornish hedge

As we walked along, clusters of sea-foam blew towards us, decorating the ground and hedges like blobs of washing up bubbles. In summer, this must be a perfect walk with skylarks trilling overhead, while seabirds such as fulmar, razorbill and guillemot nest on the cliffs.

Walking down a gully, over a stream and up the other side, I noticed that the water poured down onto the beach but the wind was blowing most of it inwards and upwards, like a persistent shower of fine rain. Down below us waves boomed into caves, sounding like a lighthouse fog warning.

Continuing along the coastal footpath, heading inland again, through a kissing gate, we passed a fenced off area with a sign saying 'Private land. Rare birds protection area including corn buntings and skylarks. Please keep to coastal footpath'. There was no sign of any skylarks or corn buntings, but if they'd got any sense they were sheltering from Storm Desmond, as it was known.

On our right a caravan park loomed up, its pale and ghostly presence sterile against the drama of the storm playing out along the coast. On our left, as we rounded the headland, three benches had been placed so that walkers could sit at various points and admire the view.

Today was not a day for doing that, so we continued towards Treyarnon Bay, past Trethias Island. Treyarnon Bay was one of Winston Graham's favourite places on the north coast; when the tide was on the make his family discovered the best waves, and would frolic in the surf on wooden boards or rubber li-los, as I remember doing as a child.

Treynarnon Bay

Today we could see no surfers – apart from the storm, there are very dangerous rip currents here at low tide, and along the rocks – but we wound our way along a muddy path leading through the holiday houses, past the whine of a machine as someone cut a tamarisk hedge. The grass and hedges were scattered with more froth from the raging sea, thrown far inland, and the hawthorn trees were covered in a thick, yellowy lichen.

Winter is perhaps the best time to see Treyarnon Bay, as we had it to ourselves. Today magnificent Atlantic rollers swept into the bay leaving a massive apron of glistening, golden sand. There are also plenty of caves to explore, and it's a short walk from Constantine Bay to the north, with its wonderful marine wildlife.

We crossed another stream that bisects the cove by way of a large wooden pallet that someone had thoughtfully laid so that people could cross the water without getting soaked feet. Treyarnon Bay didn't exist back in Poldark times, having been built relatively recently in 1988 by Sir Thomas Kenedy, making this one of the newest beaches in Cornwall. However, I could see it as a place where Demelza would have walked to from Nampara, with Garrick, and later brought the children for picnics and to swim. Ross might have joined them, to build a huge sandcastle as the tide was coming in, and lift the children on top of it, listen to their cries of delight as the tide lapped around the sand, and the castle began to crumble.

There is a cafe here in summer, but everything was shut on this December morning, so we headed inland, away from the beach, back along the road, past several houses with new slate roofs, and another beautifully built Cornish hedge that impressed Fiona greatly. Massive pine trees towered over slate roofed new houses, while palm trees and tamarisk hedges graced the gardens.

As we walked along, we saw a minute lone pink and purple trainer in the hedge, making us wonder who had lost it – and why didn't the parents notice? We wandered past Lucerne Meadow caravan park on our right then further along came to Treyarnon House, which is in fact two cottages side by side, but looked just how I imagined Nampara would. A welcoming, unpretentious house; somewhere for Ross and Demelza to come home to where muddy feet and dirty clothes wouldn't matter, but there would be a fire and something to eat awaiting.

Further on we found Treyarnon Bay Farm Cottages, which although not quite Nampara, looked the perfect place to stay – I made a note for future reference. At a T-junction past the cottages, we turned right and headed back south along the road. It was a relief to be out of the strong wind, so we relaxed and admired more examples of Cornish walling, the tamarisk hedges, and a wealth of unseasonal valerian. Looking over to our left, a screech of gulls circled over a field, and we wondered what they were doing – were they just discussing the weather, or was it a gulls' convention?

At a wooden five barred gate, we followed a Public Footpath sign on our right into a field of long grass that Moll loved, with some elderly hay bales in the corner, down to a stream with a tiny slate bridge, over a wooden stile and into another field. This cuts the corner off the road, and looking over to the field full of gulls, we saw a murmuration of starlings – thousands of them swooping and screaming in the skies, battling against the gulls.

We watched these birds for about ten minutes, circling and calling, while we sat on a fence and ate apples, marvelling at nature and I fed my apple core to

Moll. Suitably refreshed, but none the wiser when it came to bird life, we crossed over the stile back onto the road and turned right.

Walking past Trethias Farm and stables, we noticed a few rather wet looking horses – the weather this winter has been the wettest since records began. This road winds quietly along, past a spate of camping and holiday businesses – or bungaloweczema as Quiller Couch called it. We noted how many barns are now holiday lets, how many farms are now holiday centres, and how many fields are now caravan parks. Winston Graham would not have approved!

Still, Fiona sang as we walked along, and we passed a quiet and unexpected pond, surrounded by depressed looking winter gunnera, where three mallards swam busily. Apart from the holiday businesses and the occasional farm, this windswept part of Cornwall is largely devoid of buildings, and the fields provide a safe resting place for the corn bunting, which is making a comeback. Today we saw fields of crows, rooks and gulls, with the odd buzzard hovering ahead, eyes bent on its possible prey, no doubt a speck on the grass.

Coming to a T-junction, with the Tredrea Inn opposite, we turned right which led back to Porthcothan and the car park. This part of the Cornish coast

Porthcothan

boasts of being one of the most beautiful stretches of coastline to be found anywhere in the world. Even on a stormy day in December, I wouldn't argue with that.

The relationship between Ross and Demelza is also a stormy one. She doesn't apologise for who she is, which Ross admires, but she is headstrong – just as Ross is – and they can both be stubborn.

The growth in their relationship takes both by surprise. Gradually he starts to notice her intelligence, warmth and hard work, and the relationship begins to take on a life of its own. Demelza is a scrupulously honest person, and this is a trait that Ross particularly admires, being surrounded by many who are dishonest.

I like to think of this cove as the place they would go to be private. To swim in secret or hunt in the rock pools, unobserved. To walk across the cool sands and watch the gannets dive into the water.

This is Porthcothan. Nampara Cove. Come and see for yourselves.

WALK NINE
GUNWALLOE
The shipwreck walk

The famous shipwreck scenes at the end of the 2015 TV series were filmed at Gunwalloe and took place at the end of *Demelza*, the second Poldark book. At this point in the story, Demelza was struggling to fight off a terrible fever that had taken the lives of many Cornish people, including her precious daughter, Julia. Ross was beside himself, fearing he would lose Demelza as well. After caring for her for three days and nights without sleep, he finally had to bury his daughter, while storms raged outside.

Gunwalloe Cove *photograph: C Buller*

The day after Julia's funeral, a ship was spotted, drifting in on the beach, having lost all her sails. It was the *Queen Charlotte*, belonging to Ross's arch enemies, the Warleggans. Realising that she would be carrying food, he told the local miners, who would be able to enjoy the pickings: Ross felt guilty that he had not been able to feed those who came to Julia's funeral.

Ross joined the others on the beach, trying to make sure the spoils were divided fairly: pilchards, rum, corn, a dead pig, a basket of coal. By the afternoon, some 500 people, most of whom had been drinking, had gathered on the beach to claim their share. Ross swam out to the ship to see if he could save any crew, to no avail.

He was about to return home when another ship was wrecked further along the beach, just as the miners from Illogan arrived. The progress of the *Pride of Madras* had been followed by the miners as she came round Gurnard's Head, so they were ready and waiting for her, fuelled by hours spent drinking that afternoon. By early evening, 7,000 people had gathered on the beach, dragging out any valuable cargo from the ship, while some lay drunk and senseless, and many were fighting for the booty. A few soldiers from the ship made it to shore, and Ross offered them shelter. There was no choice but to leave the looters on the beach: there were too many, deranged and dangerous with drink, to argue with. Ross returned to Nampara with the crew, better to check on Demelza's progress.

Winston Graham's descriptions of the shipwrecks, and of the scenes of destruction, are vivid and compelling, and Gunwalloe lends itself to this sense of drama and wild beauty. Stand on the beach and witness the raw violence of nature; imagine the deranged miners ransacking the debris from the ships. What I find fascinating is that these double wrecks and the rioting miners on the beach actually happened on Perranporth beach in 1778.

Directions

The day we arrived at Gunwalloe was a wild, windy but warm afternoon late in October. Fiona and I travelled south from Helston past RNAS Culdrose airbase, turned right, following the signs for Gunwalloe, and then for Church Cove, where we parked in a National Trust pay and display car park near Winnianton Farm. Winnianton Manor was built on the site of one of the largest and most important Neolithic settlements in Cornwall; it owned more land than any other manor in Cornwall or Devon in 1086, and was the place where locals came to pay their taxes to the king.

What you need to know	
Distance	4 miles approximately
Allow	3 hours, including refreshment stop
Suggested Map	OS Explorer 103 The Lizard
Starting point	Winnianton Farm car park; grid reference SW 659208
Terrain	Hilly in places, coastal footpath very close to cliff edge
Nearest refreshments	Halzephron Inn. Cafe at Church Cove open Easter, then from Whitsun to end of September, 11am-5pm depending on weather
Public transport	Bus 36 or 37 from Helston ; minibus 323 from Helston
Of interest	St Winwalloe Church; Dollar Cove; Church Cove; Gunwalloe Cove
Facilities	Public toilets near car park open at Easter, then Whitsun to end of September. Dogs allowed on Dollar Cove all year round.
Parking	£3.50 at time of walking

From the car park, walk down towards the sea and the first cove on the right is called Jangye-ryn, or Dollar Cove; a rough beach with rock formations of special interest to geologists because the contorted strata of the cliffs represent a thousand years of tectonic plate movement. Locals and archaeologists have seen evidence of ancient buildings eroding from the cliff for some time now. These belong to a very rare example of early medieval settlement, now buried by the sand dunes, dating from between 600 and 900 AD.

This is where the Spanish ship, *San Salvador*, was wrecked in 1669. The ship was reputed to have been carrying two tons of silver dollars, and some of these are still supposed to wash up on the coast after storms – hence the name Dollar Cove.

Round the corner from Dollar Cove, and separated by a 60 foot promontory, is Church Cove, and the church of St Winwalloe. There has been a church here since Domesday times, although the current church, set back from the beach,

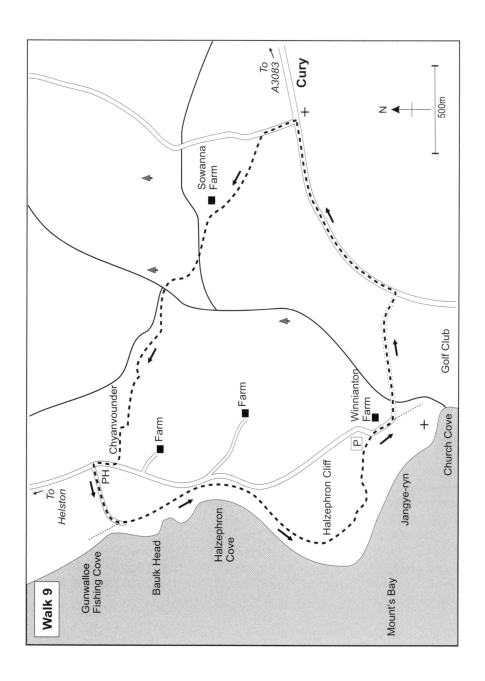

Walk 9

Gunwalloe
Fishing Cove

Baulk Head

Halzephron
Cove

Mount's Bay

Church Cove

Jangye-ryn

Halzephron Cliff

Winnianton
Farm

P

PH

Chyanvounder

To
Helston

Farm

Farm

Sowanna
Farm

To
A3083

Cury

Golf Club

N

500m

Dollar Cove

was built in the 14th or 15th century and has a small Norman tower which nestles on the inner bank of the headland, while the main body of the church, and the ancient graveyard, are next door. Being almost on the beach, when there are spring tides and high winds, the spray soaks the front door.

St Winwalloe was born in Brittany in the 6th century, of Cornish parentage: in the porch you will see a figure of him, and the church contains timbers from the Portuguese galleon *St Anthony* which was wrecked in the cove on 19th January, 1527. This was the flagship of King John III of Portugal's fleet, and was not only carrying copper and silver ingots but also the dowry of Princess Katherine, bride of King John III and sister of the Holy Roman Emperor, Charles V. Because the seabed off Gunwalloe is formed of rocky gullies, and storms can cause huge shifts of sediment, this can mean large changes in the seabed depth. Consequently, the next morning, the ship was stranded in just six feet of water. As only half the crew survived, they weren't able to protect the cargo from Cornish locals, and most of it disappeared.

The exact location of this wreck wasn't discovered until 1981 when a copper ingot was found by a shellfish diver, and when another was washed up on the beach, records were matched and the wreck site revealed.

Leaving Church cove, we marvelled at a group of young children in shorts playing on the beach (it was autumn half term), walked back towards the public toilets and cafe (shut in winter) and turned right to cross a small bridge surrounded by bamboo, over the National Trust Towans or golf course. Taking note of golfers on either side of us, we walked up a small road with grass growing up the middle, while a chaffinch chirped at us from a bramble bush.

Past the Mullion Golf Club Teaching Academy, we continued over the hill to the Golf Club Pro Shop, narrowly missed being hit by several golf balls, and turned left along the road, towards Cury. It took a while, as we kept passing massive blackberries, which we had to eat. They were very late in the season, but beautifully dark, rich and sweet – and MollieDog ate her fair share, too.

Passing Chymder Cottages and farm on our left, we arrived in Cury (Churchtown), where we could see the church on our right, and the hedges bursting with voluptuous, if out of season, red valerian. The summer drone of a lawnmower accompanied us as we continued, turning first left just before the church, into another minor road signposted 'Milliwarne ¾', while a helicopter (presumably from RNAS Culdrose) hovered ahead.

With the small cemetery on our left, flanked by a row of cherry trees, we walked for a few minutes before finding a large field entrance and a stone stile on our left, near a five barred gate, and a public footpath sign leading into a field. Here, we found a sign saying 'Gunwalloe 1½' and a field full of cows, so Moll had to go back on the lead. We walked cautiously across the middle of the field, towards the buildings ahead in the distance, when I noticed a bull on our right. I have to say I'm not too comfortable around male cattle of that size. With horns. Looking at you, licking their lips.

However, Fiona was made of sterner stuff and strode forth, with Moll on the lead, while I brought up a wimpish rear, clutching camera, map and tape recorder. "The thing is," she said, "if you avoid cows, you end up taking huge detours, and that would just be really confusing if you're trying to give accurate directions." She's quite right, of course, but I was very glad she was going first, while my eyes darted around the hedges, seeking a quick exit in the event of being chased.

"He was lovely", said Fiona, when we were safely out of the field, peering at the bull from the safety of a five barred gate. Even I had to agree – he had chestnut brown curly hair and quite a placid expression. "He'd obviously had his fill," she continued cheerfully. Presumably she was right, as we lived to tell the tale.

We went wrong here, owing to lack of signage, and Fiona ended up manhandling a very heavy iron gate and ending up in a pond. "I want royalties," she muttered, wading through the muddy water, "and I'm not afraid to ask." (Make note.)

What we should have done was continue across the bull field until we came to join a farm drive and walked past Sowanna farmyard where we found a waymark sign on the left by the farmhouse. To our relief, we found another public footpath on our right and headed down a grassy path with beech trees on either side of us, till we reached a stone stile, climbed up and over a hedge into a large field full of more cattle.

"I'm the one with the dog," said Fiona, seizing Moll's lead. "I should be scared." Thankfully she wasn't, and, steering clear of inquisitive cows, we made our way down the right hand side of the field towards the bottom – it was quite a steep hill, with reeds and a stream at the end. Here we found a wooden stile over a fence and clambered over that onto a wooden boardwalk with wild mint growing in abundance.

Over another stile and section of boardwalk, we arrived in another field, with no cows (at the time of writing) but it was very muddy so do wear wellies. Continuing diagonally over the field we followed a rough path to another stile, another field, down through a little valley where gorse and bracken had recently been cleared. It was very quiet and still here, and we headed off to the left, seeing another boardwalk, over a boggy patch, and a succession of boardwalks and wooden stiles. Over to our left, a silent heron took off, grey wings flapping slowly in the stillness of the afternoon.

A stream ran through this very flat area of low lying nettles and damp ground, and we reached a Pooh Sticks bridge, then a few more stiles into a field where a house was being built. Here there were more cows but they were fenced off, so we skirted to the left of a man made pond, waded through a very muddy section, (Fiona very smug in her wellies), through a reedy part, and over a stile to find another path heading uphill into a field. We continued heading uphill to a waymark sign on the left.

As we waded through a boggy part, Fiona looked around. "It's a lovely walk though, isn't it?" she said. I agreed, as we were free of bovines, and we walked up a stone track to another waymark sign on the right and into another grassy track. This led us past sloe bushes and blackberries to a very quiet, stony path covered in sycamore leaves and nettles. At the top of this path we turned right, heading downhill.

The path continued down to the right along a boggy section, past a derelict cottage with cob walls that had eroded over the years, while the path curved round to the left and led us up to a large field that we walked diagonally across, finally seeing the houses of Gunwalloe ahead of us on the horizon (it felt like a long mile and a half). Moll loved this huge expanse of grass, and cantered across it like a Grand National runner, ears streaming behind her.

The sun was beginning to set when we got here, casting elegant shadows across the grass. Finally we climbed over a wooden stile and gate and arrived at a grassy lane and into the road at Gunwalloe, past a few houses where we turned right to the Halzephron Inn and enjoyed a very welcome ginger beer and some free dog biscuits for Moll.

Halzephron Inn

Refreshed, we turned first left almost opposite the pub, down a road leading to Gunwalloe Fishing Cove where children and dogs scampered along the sand, screaming and laughing as the sun continued to sink, casting lengthening shadows like fairytale fingers over the bouncing waves.

Turning south towards Park Bean, a house on the edge of the cliff, surrounded by tamarisk trees, we skirted round to the left and continued up the increasingly steep coastal path, until we came to Halzephron House up on the left, which was the original home of Halzephron Herbs and Spices. Just past here, in someone's garden, we saw a life sized carved wooden angel on a plinth overlooking the sea. It was such a wonderful spectacle; the angel's outspread arms giving thanks to a splendid day.

Further along the cliff path, we came to a National Trust sign saying 'Halzephron Cliff' next to a layby full of vans and people with camera equipment, and wondered if they might be filming Poldark! Halzephron comes from 'als' meaning Hell in Cornish, and 'ephron' from 'yfarn' meaning cliff – if you look down as you walk, you will see why these cliffs got their name. The footpath is well trodden along here, with hawthorn hedges on the seaward side, and a few of the last blackberries.

The views over Mounts Bay from here are superb – to Loe Bar and Porthleven, further round to Penzance and St Michael's Mount, with the Penwith moors behind them. Looking down as we walked, the sea was a milky green, swirling and foaming beneath us. If you are lucky you may be able to see a Cornish chough feeding on the cliffs below you, or maybe a kestrel, peregrine or raven.

The footpath meanders along the edge of the cliffs here, so if you suffer from vertigo, as I do, don't look down! I concentrated on the flowers: a few ox eye daisies, and the last of the cow parsley, nodding white heads at us as we passed. The wind hit us as the path turned south east, and on the headland ahead of us is a large, imposing cream building that I think should be in the next James Bond film. It was in fact the Poldhu Hotel, built for Marconi workers, and is now a care home.

View from Halzephron cliffs

Looking down to Loe Bar

Poldhu means 'black cove' in Cornish, referring to the famous Serpentine rock local to this area, which looks like snakeskin when polished. However, the Poldhu Wireless Station is most famous because Marconi transmitted the first transatlantic radio message from it, on December 12th, 1901, to a receiving station in St John's, Newfoundland. Marconi used Poldhu again in 1923 and 1924, for shortwave radio experiments, resulting in the development of the Beam Wireless Service for the British Post Office.

Poldhu Station operated until 1933; the site was cleared in 1935 and six acres given to the National Trust in 1937 with the rest of the site added in 1960. In 2001 a new museum/meeting building called the Marconi Centre was opened nearby.

From Halzephron Cliff, we continued along the path until we returned to Winnianton car park, arriving as the sun set.

Winston Graham excelled at capturing the drama of the Cornish coastline in the Poldark books, and this area demonstrates the rugged, dangerous and beautiful nature of Cornwall at its best.

The last time few times I've visited Gunwalloe, it has been with grey skies and a stiff breeze: a storm brewing. Anyone can see how perilous the coast is here; how ships could be wrecked on these rocks in minutes. Stand on the beach for a moment and listen – to the roar of the hungry seas, and the wind screaming in your ears. If you look hard enough, you can perhaps see the gathering hordes, drunken, starving and desperate, clamouring on the beach. Is that a glint of gold in the sand? This is true Poldark country.

WALK TEN
CAERHAYS CASTLE
Home of the Trevanion family

One December morning, Mel and I left Falmouth to meet her aunt, Janet, at Heligan Gardens before walking at Caerhays (or Craze as the locals call it). Janet was sitting in the outside seating area looking a little hesitant. "I don't want to interfere with your walking plans," she said, fumbling in her bag, "but I've got a voucher here, and I wondered if you'd like some lunch."

She pulled out a voucher for the Heligan cafe and we both grinned – we couldn't have had a better start to the outing. The food at Heligan is very fresh, extremely tasty and varied. Several tables were occupied by folks wearing festive hats and eating Christmas dinner, but our soup, fresh cheese scones and pineapple fruit cake was just as good, if not better, so do give the food a try if you have time.

Directions
To get to Caerhays from St Austell, head south west on Carlyon Road, drive along the A390 then turn left onto the B3287 and follow the signs to Caerhays.

From Heligan, we followed Janet round the twisty, muddy, narrow lanes with pheasants wandering aimlessly along the road, and suddenly, rounding a corner, was a small (by castle standards) fairytale castle set back from the road with a lake and sloping lawns in front of it. It's so surprising to find it here, and so splendidly perfect, that I smile and my heart gives a skip every time I see it.

In 1807 the Trevanion family commissioned the famous architect, John Nash, to build Caerhays (translated as 'enclosed castle') on the grounds of the old manor house that had been in the Arundell family since the early Middle Ages. Caerhays is one of the few remaining examples of Nash's castles, and has only

What you need to know	
Distance	1½ miles
Allow	1½ hours
Suggested Map	OS Explorer 105 Falmouth & Mevagissey
Starting point	Porthluney beach; grid ref: SW 974413
Terrain	A few steep hills
Nearest refreshments	Caerhays castle, beach cafe in summer; cafe at Portholland
Public transport	Nearest railway station St Austell
Of interest	Caerhays Castle – tea room, shop and gardens open mid Feb to June – first see website for details. Conducted tours of the castle are available by arrangement
Facilities	Public toilets at each cove, and cafes at Porthluney and East Porthholland (seasonal only). Porthluney beach dog friendly all year round. Parking free in winter, check for prices in summer

ever been lived in by two families. The Trevanions, who owned property all over Cornwall, were bankrupted by the project and in 1840 they fled to France to escape their debts. In 1854, the then derelict house was bought by Michael Wiliams, from Burncoose, and has remained in the family ever since.

Looking like a Norman castle, Caerhays was built of rough stone quarried locally. The front entrance, 160 ft (49 m) in length, faces south and is raised on a terrace. Parts of the original manor remain, including the ancient chapel and an old walkway to the sea, called the Watchhouse Walk.

The Williams introduced a park and lake into the gardens, which cover almost 120 acres, and in 1907, funded a camellia trip to the Himalayas. The two explorers, Ernest Wilson and George Forest, brought back rare camellias and rhododendrons. Since then, the x Williamsii Camellia, which was first grown here at Caerhays, has become one of the most valuable hybrid shrubs ever produced. Magnolias were also introduced, and today Caerhays is home to the Plant Heritage National Collection of Magnolias, containing over 600 species and named hybrids from all over the world. This is the largest

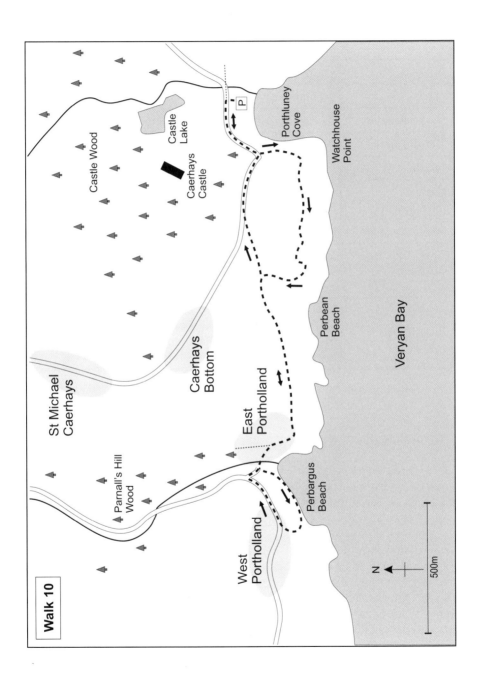

Walk 10

St Michael
Caerhays

Castle Wood

Castle
Lake

Caerhays
Castle

Caerhays
Bottom

Parnall's Hill
Wood

East
Portholland

West
Portholland

Perbargus
Beach

Perbean
Beach

Perbean
Beach

Watchhouse
Point

Porthluney
Cove

P

Veryan Bay

N

500m

Caerhays Castle

magnolia collection in England, and has won many gold medals at Chelsea Flower Show.

In *The Loving Cup*, the tenth Poldark novel, Jeremy, the oldest of the Poldark children, falls in love with Cuby Trevanion, who lives with her impoverished family at Caerhays Castle. Having overspent on the house, the family need Cuby to marry a rich man, and Jeremy, despite being from a good Cornish family, is not considered rich enough. So she declines Jeremy's love and offer of marriage, and, being a sensitive soul, he is heartbroken.

George Warleggan steps in, deciding that Cuby – or rather, Caerhays Castle – would be a suitable addition to the Warleggan properties. For the sum of twenty thousand pounds, paid to the Trevanions, he would establish Valentine (his stepson) as the husband of a girl of an ancient family and therefore in possession of one of the noblest houses in Cornwall. Just to make sure Valentine would be sole master of the house, he would pay Trevanion an extra thousand to leave the castle within a year of the couple marrying.

Jeremy hears of this plan and is in despair. Desperate for money to impress the Trevanions, he takes drastic action. Together with two other friends, they rob a stagecoach delivering money, but he is disgusted with himself, with his friends and with the idea that he has let his family down.

He does his best to forget Cuby, but after 18 months of a broken heart, and unable to face her forthcoming marriage to Valentine, he decides to enlist as a soldier and fight in Holland. He feels he has led a privileged and cosseted life, and this will be a chance for him to grow up; to become a man.

So far so good, but in true Winston Graham style, George Warleggan's plans are thwarted by Valentine secretly marrying Selina Pope, a young widow. When Jeremy returns on leave, Ross urges him to go and see Cuby and persuade her to marry him. At first astonished at Ross's suggestion, Jeremy finally takes his advice: he takes two horses to Caerhays, climbs over the walls and into the castle where he hides in Cuby's bedroom. With the element of surprise in his favour, she realises that she does love him, so he persuades her to accompany him by coach to London and marry there, then travel direct to Brussels for him to rejoin his regiment.

The gamble pays off, and Ross and Demelza are rewarded for their liberated thinking by an ecstatic letter from Jeremy telling them his news in detail – as a blissfully happy husband.

When we arrived at Caerhays – by van, rather than riding – the car park at Porthluney beach, next to Caerhays, was free at the time of walking, but check prices in season. There is also a cafe set back from the beach in the summer, but again this was shut for the winter. This was Mel's nearest beach when she was growing up, "though we only came here when it was raining," she explained. "Dad (a farmer) was always harvesting if the weather was good."

Today it was free of rain, and the tide was coming in; long Atlantic rollers sweeping over the dry sand. In the second series of Poldark in the 1970s, Ross galloped across Porthluney beach, and if you close your eyes, you can almost hear the hoof beats drumming on the sand, see the horse's tail floating out as he rides by, exhilarated by the wind and the tide.

But there was only us on the beach, so, heading out of the car park and turning left up the road, we rounded a bend to see Caerhays Castle, nestling in Grade II listed parkland. A covey of pheasants stared as the near gale force

Cliffs towards Porthluney

wind pushed us up the hill. "The castle and gardens are open in spring," said Janet, "and the magnolias are amazing."

The narrow road winds steeply uphill, round the corner where the road must have been carved through a wall of slate, streaked with varied colours of purple and umber orange with magnificent ropes of ivy threaded through them. On our left an old folly was being restored behind metal barriers: we wondered what it would look like when finished.

At the top of this hill is a Public Footpath sign to 'East Portholland 1 mile', so we climbed up some steps, through a kissing gate onto the headland. On our left was a tall pine tree known to her family as Mel's tree, as it was one of the first things she painted. We headed downhill towards the sea, passing a lot of very windswept trees, while Moll did a few somersaults in excitement, and hurtled through the grass, relieved to be out of the van.

The wild splendour of Veryan Bay stretched out in front of us on this stormy day with Gull Rock a shadowy isle rising out of the turbulent seas. This was

View towards Gull Rock

true Poldark weather – I was almost on the lookout for a few schooners about to be shipwrecked on the rocks below. The sea was a tormented, bluey-green, with wild white horses, as gulls swirled above us, buffeted by the elements.

Following the coastal footpath, stunted trees and hawthorn bushes were moulded inland by the prevailing south westerly winds, while on our right was scrubby moorland, like my brother's closely cropped red hair when he was little.

We continued through another kissing gate and looked up on our right, inland, to see a small hut which is now used by the Caerhays Estate for weddings. We climbed up the almost vertical hill towards it – "My legs are saying we don't normally do this!" Janet said, as we puffed upwards – to find this tiny hut, which was formerly a coastguard's lookout. Though if you did decide to marry here, you couldn't invite many guests, and as there is no glass in the windows, I should pick a calm and warm day. But the views are stunning, through the arched stone windows from Nare Head and Gull Rock in the West to Dodman Point in the east. On clear days you can even see the Lizard Peninsular.

Leaving the hut behind us, we walked along the top of the field to a wooden five barred gate with a faded yellow waymarker sign, walked through that onto a small muddy path slightly sheltered from the strong winds. Long grass brushed our feet and Moll's tummy, while saffron yellow gorse flowers and a few pink campions provided the only colour on a grey day.

Along here we passed a wooden bench dedicated to 'John Warrington 1950-2008 Loved and remembered always'. Those benches always cause a catch in my throat, and looking out over the seas rolling in on this blustery, Poldark day, I thought what a lovely place to put a bench. I bet Cuby would have put one there in memory of Jeremy.

View from the hut

A small quarry on our right housed a few home made swings made of branches and blue twine – I was tempted to have a go but they looked a bit frail. We stopped here to take pictures of East Portholland in the distance – this beach was used as Roscoff in Brittany in the second 1970s series, transforming the boathouses and fish sheds (now converted into housing) into a corner of a French fishing port.

As we approached, the path wound inland, down towards Portholland, and I noticed a cluster of pine trees on the opposite field, growing at an astonishing angle. We passed under a tunnel of holly (with berries) intertwined with brambles, before turning left, down towards the beach. Past a huge granite gatepost and several interesting gates made of driftwood leading to an allotment, we noticed a hebe bush in full flower.

The full force of the south westerly wind hit us as we reached the beach where the tide was out revealing a smooth expanse of wet sand, with six seagulls standing like sentries, facing seawards.

East Portholland

Here we saw a sign 'Pebbles Cafe and Crafts open Tuesday to Saturday'. This is the smallest post office I've ever seen, selling home made knitted hats, bunting and mittens with a tiny cafe next door boasting a minute woodburner and the biggest tabby cat I've seen for a long time.

Walking round here we felt as if we'd stepped back in time – it's completely unspoilt: no tourist cafes or ice cream kiosks here. Just a row of fishermen's cottages, a converted boathouse or two and a red phone box decorated with tinsel.

We walked round to West Portholland, along a concrete path above the beach, then a difficult scramble over steep rocks onto the beach. However, you could always walk via the road which is safer, and the way we came back. If you do come over the rocks, take note of the tide – it came in very quickly the day we were there, meaning you wouldn't be able to return that way. Luxury accommodation awaits you here, as part of the Caerhays Estate, and a converted Methodist chapel near the road.

We turned right here, back along the road, signed 'Coast Path East Portholland ⅓ mile', passing another row of cottages, and more holiday accommodation. At a junction we then turned right, back into East Portholland where we noticed a pond with several geese, and some public toilets (always a winner for me). There is also a private car park with an honesty box.

We returned the way we had come, noticing the sand below us is really dark – there is a lot of slate among the cliffs here, making for dramatic pictures. We walked back along the sheltered path as far as the wedding hut, where we passed through a five barred gate, onto the road where we turned right and continued back to Porthluney. There is a large layby here so if you wished to park here and get married, or walk along the cliffs down to Portholland, or back to Porthluney, this would be a good option.

I have a special affinity with this area, as if I have some former, innate knowledge of it. For me it has a sense of familiarity, even while it is unfamiliar.

West Portholland

I love the fact that nothing of this part of the coast is spoilt – Porthluney and Portholland are almost as they would have been in Poldark's times. It's wonderful to hear the squawk of pheasants, see dogs cavorting over the beaches and a shoot going on in the fields by the castle when we came back. Apart from the Land Rovers, nothing much had changed.

Porthluney was also used in the second 1970s series as the beach where Morwenna and the young Geoffrey Charles meet Drake Carne and they go to the Holy Well together. This is the start of a dangerous love that causes much unhappiness, and involves many people before finding a joyful resolution.

But Poldark – and therefore, Cornwall, contains the vicissitudes of life: the unhappiness, the joys, the bitterness, and transforms them into a profound and long lasting love. This is what Winston Graham evokes so well, and in the case of Porthluney – of Morwenna and Drake, and of Caerhays – of Cuby and Jeremy, it is well worth waiting for.

Go to this wonderful castle, explore the grounds and admire the magnolias and camellias. Walk along the sloping cliffs, breathe that strong salty air, listen to the indignant squawk of the pheasants, and immerse yourself in true Poldark country.

WALK ELEVEN
CHARLESTOWN
also known as Truro

In the 2015 Poldark TV series, Charlestown often stands in for Truro, as well as being used for various fishing and fishmonger scenes. Fishing in Cornwall in the 17th and 18th centuries was one of the main industries, while pilchard fishing and processing was a thriving industry from 1750 to around 1880, after which it went into an almost terminal decline. Fishing was not only a vital source of income for many families, but for many mining families, a pilchard glut could feed them for weeks.

The marriage of Verity Poldark to Andrew Blamey was also filmed on one of the beautiful tall ships in Charlestown harbour. This happy event marked the

Tall ships in Charlestown harbour

end of a long and traumatic courtship, involving battles with Verity's father and brother, both of whom disapproved of the man she loved.

The ancient harbour of Charlestown grew out of the tiny fishing village of West Polmear, where pilchards were processed. Charles Rashleigh began building the harbour and dock in 1791 and the first dock gates were completed in 1799. He also planned the village, and the broad road from the harbour to Mount Charles. In 1793 a gun battery was built to the west of the harbour mouth, in defence against possible French attacks. In 1799 the locals asked his permission to rename the place Charles's Town. The port was built to facilitate the transport of copper from nearby mines.

What you need to know	
Distance	4 miles approximately
Allow	2 hours
Suggested Map	OS Explorer 107 St Austell & Liskeard
Starting point	Porthpean car park; grid reference SW 031507
Terrain	A few steep hills, otherwise easy going
Nearest refreshments	Several pubs and cafes in Charlestown; cafe at Porthpean
Public transport	Western Greyhound 525 from St Austell. Nearest railway station St Austell
Of interest	Charlestown harbour and tall ships; Charlestown Shipwreck and Heritage Centre
Facilities	Toilets at Porthpean and Charlestown. Dog ban Easter Day to October first on all beaches

Directions

On a beautiful morning in late February, which also happened to be my birthday, Fiona and I headed off to Charlestown. Coming from the St Austell direction on the A390, turn right at the traffic lights signposted to Porthpean, Duporth and Hospital. Continue past the hospital, turn first left signposted 'Porthpean Beach ½ mile' and continue downhill to the car park which is on the right with an honesty box asking for £3 (at the time of walking).

From the car park, we walked straight ahead towards the sea, relishing the warm sunshine. Passing Porthpean Sailing Club, we saw families with children and dogs digging in the sand, building castles and running along the beach, while one family had lit a barbecue and was frying sausages.

Pulling Moll away, with twitching nostrils (and that was just us), we walked along the beach, while lazy waves swished towards us leaving lacy imprints on the sand as seagulls weaved and soared above us. St Austell Bay lay before us dressed in navy, turquoise and a sea green: a perfect birthday welcome.

You can either walk along the beach, north towards Charlestown, or along the concrete walkway past Porthpean Boathouse and the cafe, which was shut being winter, until you come to the coastal footpath on the left leading uphill. Rejoicing in the Wedgewood blue skies, we struggled up this increasingly steep hill and paused to take photographs and admire the Mediterranean looking waters, out to the red and white striped beacon of Gribbin Head.

Coming to a lookout tower, we turned right and walked through a quiet, gently shaded wooded area dotted with primroses, and benches for walkers to enjoy the view. To our right (south) we could see Gerrans Point and Black Head in the misty sunshine. Walking past the second bench, we continued along this footpath, under an arch of trees, with tangles of tall brambles on either side

Porthpean beach

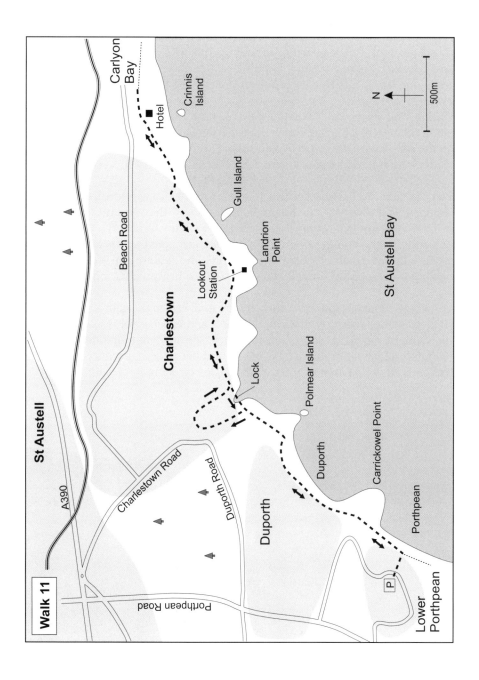

Walk 11

St Austell

A390

Charlestown Road

Porthpean Road

Duporth Road

Beach Road

Charlestown

Duporth

Lookout Station

Lock

Carlyon Bay

Hotel

Crinnis Island

Gull Island

Landrion Point

Polmear Island

St Austell Bay

Carrickowel Point

Duporth

Porthpean

Lower Porthpean

P

N

500m

Duporth beach

and pussy willow announcing spring. At Carrickowel Point we passed another picnic area with tables and a bench, looking out over Duporth beach. Further round, to the east, the long expanse of Carlyon Bay beach stretched in the sunshine while the waves thundered below us and the sea glinted turquoise, inky dark and pale blue.

The path petered out so we retraced our steps to the last picnic area where we turned right along the coastal footpath past a sign saying 'No Tipping'. There were many modern houses on our left, separated by a fence, with elegant daffodils nodding in the spring sunshine and the startling pink of a camellia poking through. There's a wooded area on our right where trees had recently been felled, and further on, we ignored the path that leads down to Duporth beach and continued along the footpath over a little bridge. Along the path were lots of three cornered leek: I always used to think these were sort of snowdrops but they are actually part of the onion family, "and they're great if you chop up the leaves and put them in an omelette", said Fiona, who knows these things.

The path twists round below the houses and gardens, separated by a green wire fence, and we noticed the first celandines smiling up at us. There's a steep drop from the path down to the beach below, but the hedge on the seaward side protected us, to my relief, as vertigo still lingers on occasions.

It was so warm out of the easterly wind that we both stopped to shed our coats, noticing the trees arching in, landwards, bent by the prevailing south westerly winds. "Isn't nature clever?" said Fiona. "The trees provide a canopy when it's really hot and when it's winter, they let all the light in, which is what you need when it's cold." I looked at her. "Very profound", I said, and we both laughed.

Passing through a kissing gate with a sign warning, 'Danger cliff erosion, keep to footpath', we continued with a field on our left, separated by a fence, and came to Crinnis Cliff Battery, otherwise known as Charlestown Battery.

Volunteers from Rashleigh's estate formed an artillery company that lasted until 1860, when the original four 18-pound cannons were replaced by 24-pound models.The Crinnis Cliff Volunteers became the Cornwall Artillery Volunteers, and the battery continued to be used for practice until 1898. Very little of the gunpowder magazine can still be seen, but there are stunning views over Carlyon Bay, so we enjoyed those before descending a steep hill punctuated by a series of shallow wooden steps leading down to Charlestown.

A large crow croaked over our heads while we passed through an old metal kissing gate, past a row of coastguard cottages on our left, and a sunlit view of Charlestown harbour, with an incoming tide.

Charlestown harbour and beach

Despite competition from the port at Pentewan, which opened in 1826, and from Par, which opened shortly afterwards, Charlestown prospered from exporting china clay until the onset of the First World War.

The harbour was designed for small sailing vessels, and an awkward turn was needed to avoid the protruding end of the outer harbour. Following the widening of the entrance and the fitting of new gates in 1971, ships of up to 600 tons were able to enter the harbour, but only at high tide, and a system of ropes was used to manoeuvre vessels through the gates. By the 1990s, the size of vessels used for the transport of china clay had outgrown the harbour, and the last commercial load of clay left Charlestown in 2000, with exports of china clay leaving Cornwall through Par or the deep water port at Fowey instead.

In 1994 the harbour was bought by Square Sail as a base for their sailing ships and for film sets such as the 2015 Poldark television series. In 2015 the business (including the harbour, workshops and ships) was bought by Square Sail Ventures Limited, a full service production company that designs, builds and stages events worldwide. The *Phoenix*, usually used for filming, is a 112 ft long, two masted brig that was built in 1929 and converted to an 18th century brig in 1996.

Some of the outdoor scenes involving Verity Poldark's romance with Andrew Blamey were filmed round Charlestown Harbour, standing in for Truro. Verity Poldark is a kind and caring woman who has spent most of her life being a dutiful daughter to her father Charles, but her family take her for granted and she rarely goes out. Verity and Ross are very close: he has always treated her equally and is on her side, whereas she feels her brother Francis is not.

When Ross returns from war, this allows her to enter society, and at a dance she meets Captain Andrew Blamey, and they fall instantly in love. But it turns out that Blamey is known for his volatile temper, which resulted in the death of his pregnant wife. Now a reformed alcoholic and ridden with guilt, Blamey wishes to marry Verity, who is willing to forgive him, but Francis and their father, Charles, disapprove of Blamey and send him away.

Ross takes Demelza into Truro (Charlestown) one day to buy her a cloak and there sees Verity meeting Andrew in secret. Ross believes that Blamey's wife's death was an accident and that Blamey is a good man. Ross also wishes to see his cousin Verity happy. So he helps Verity arrange a meeting with Andrew at

Nampara. But Charles and Francis ride over to Nampara, discover the couple talking innocently, and blame Ross for his interference.

Verity claims she has the right to choose her own life, but Francis challenges Andrew to a duel. Duelling was a familiar practice among the upper classes of this time, and duels were fought with pistols or swords. They were usually motivated by the participants' desire to show their willingness to risk their lives so as to restore their honour, rather than to kill their opponent. While many disapproved of duelling, others felt it helped encourage good manners: much better to raise one's hat and avoid an argument, rather than the risk of a duel and being shot.

Despite fierce opposition from Ross and Verity, the duel goes ahead, and Francis is badly hurt. Ross saves his life, but Verity tells Andrew she realises that it is impossible for them to be together now, so he must go. Both are broken hearted at the way this has turned out.

Verity's life is in pieces, and she is resigned to staying a spinster, but Demelza is determined to bring the couple together. Secretly she manages to track Andrew Blamey down and tells him how unhappy Verity is. Finally, after a great deal of persuasion, the couple meet covertly and eventually, after a lot of soul searching, Verity agrees to elope and marry Andrew in secret. When they walk onto Andrew's ship as newly weds, it is clear that they are both happy at last.

Having discussed this part of the plot with Fiona, we reached the harbour, and she said, "As it's your birthday I'm buying you a drink." So I sat outside the pub while she disappeared inside (I do pick my friends well). I suddenly saw another very dear friend (who lives in Dorset) standing outside with her husband. They came and joined us for a drink and I sat feeling very lucky and happy.

As time was ticking on, we forced ourselves away from the pub and explored the harbour and wonderful tall ships currently moored up while a flock of doves flew overhead and settled in a line on a metal pole. There is also a Shipwreck and Heritage Centre which is worth a visit, as well as several pubs and cafes.

Walking round the harbour, we came to a coastal footpath sign indicating 'Carlyon Bay 1.5 miles', and set off up a steep gravelled path with steps at various shallow intervals, a sunny field full of sheep on our left and an old mine chimney in the distance, reminding us that mining was never far away, in Poldark times.

The scent of wild garlic was powerful here – and a welcome sign that spring is on the way, as we went through a wooded area covered with with three cornered leeks. Over the hills, we could see the Cornish Alps, as the china clay workings are known, while the path wound round to the east, and the sun shone on camellia and holly leaves, making them look almost white, they were so bright.

Coming to a tall wooden fence on our left, we passed through a wooden kissing gate and yet more signs of coastal erosion. Walking past the Porth Avallen hotel, the path dipped round to the right, to Landrion Point, where we found the National Coastwatch Institution, Charlestown Station – 'Visitors Welcome', the sign said, so we climbed the steep steps to the lookout station where Harold showed us around. It's 56 metres above sea level, so the panoramic views round St Austell bay are well worth sampling.

Doves in Charlestown harbour

It was built in the early 20th century as an auxiliary Coastguard lookout, but became redundant and was abandoned. It was rediscovered and refurbished in 2001 and finally opened as a NCI station in 2003.

Leaving Harold behind, we followed the coastal path round past a large wooden fence on our left in front of some large houses, and more cheery daffodils until we came to two large grassy areas, popular with dog walkers and their four legged friends, running up and down in the sunshine. Ahead of us was Carlyon Bay, and to our left was a collection of huge houses, some Colonial style with a Union Jack flag flying from a pole in the garden. After the grassy fields, the hexagonal shape of the Carlyon Bay Hotel appeared on our left, and here we had to turn round as we'd run out of time.

We retraced our steps to Charlestown where a bonfire had been lit near the field of sheep, and smoke drifted over the valley like a gauze veil, while a gaggle of geese squawked indignantly at some unseen interruption. Six inch wide ropes of ivy throttled some of the trees on our left, and we looked down on a sunlit Charlestown beach while blackbirds sang around us.

Reaching Charlestown harbour, instead of looping round to see the ships, we walked down a few steps to a private quay and small footbridge which we crossed over to reach the other side of the harbour below the Pier House pub we'd visited earlier. From here we picked up the coastal footpath back to Porthpean, saw the first very pale bluebells and were serenaded by robins as we reflected on what had been a perfect birthday walk. Would that Andrew and Verity, Ross and Demelza could have shared it too.

ST WINNOW AND LERRYN

The venue for

Dwight Enys and Caroline Penvenen's wedding

Ross's friend and doctor, Dwight Enys, finally married Caroline Penvenen and in the second 1970s television series, the wedding was filmed at the beautiful and secluded church of St Winnow overlooking the river Fowey.

Dwight Enys was a young doctor who also fought in America with Ross and treated his injuries. They became firm friends and Dwight proved a very conscientious, tireless and generous doctor, often working unpaid and open to innovative treatments, unlike Dr Choake, who was only too keen to bleed patients, both physically and financially. After a tragic entanglement with a young miner's wife, Dwight resolved to concentrate on his work until he met Caroline Penvenen, a young heiress.

Caroline was an orphan, raised by her rich uncle Ray. She grew into a strong willed and independent young woman, unwilling to marry the older man chosen for her and instead, falling in love with Dwight and pursuing him. Her elderly uncle thought Dwight socially unsuitable for his heiress niece; their courtship endured numerous ups and downs, including a plan to elope that misfired, which led to a massive misunderstanding and Caroline refusing to see Dwight.

Months later, broken hearted from hearing of Caroline's engagement to another man, Dwight decided to enter the Navy as a surgeon. However, Ross intervened, saw Dwight and Caroline separately and, convinced that they still loved each other, managed to persuade them to meet. The rendezvous was successful and, to Ross and Demelza's delight, the couple pledged to marry when Dwight came out of the Navy.

But, in true Poldark style, nothing was ever that simple. Dwight was involved in a naval battle near the French coast, and most of the ship's survivors, including Dwight, were taken prisoner. When Caroline heard this, she enlisted Ross's help in campaigning for Dwight's freedom. Ross and some friends sailed over to France, but found him near death yet reluctant to abandon his fellow prisoners who were also very ill. Ross persuaded him to escape, and brought him back to Cornwall where Caroline vowed to nurse him back to health and, eventually, to marry. This marriage endured more separations and the death of their first child, but their love was strong and the couple were helped by their close friends, Ross and Demelza.

What you need to know	
Distance	5 miles
Allow	3 hours at least
Suggested Map	OS Explorer 107 St Austell & Liskeard
Starting point	Lerryn car park; grid reference SX 115570
Terrain	A few steep hills
Nearest refreshments	Ship Inn shut some afternoons – check opening hours www.theshipinnlerryn.co.uk – or Lerryn River Stores
Public transport	482 bus Polruan to Bodmin. Nearest rail station Lostwithiel
Of interest	St Winnow Mill, Church at St Winnow, Ethy house
Facilities	Public toilets at Lerryn

Directions

From St Austell we drove along Slades Road to Carclaze Road, through St Blazey and continued along the A390 through Lostwithiel. Driving through the town we took a sharp right after the industrial units and followed the signs to Lerryn where we parked in the free car park on the quay.

A note here – if using this car park at spring tides, beware, as Lerryn can flood at certain times when the tides and wind are both high.

From the car park, as the tide was high, we retraced our steps the way we drove in, past Lerryn Memorial Hall, over the narrow bridge, and took a left turn after Bridge House, seeing a No Through Road sign, past several cottages and turned first left again to walk along the creek. If you are walking at low tide, opposite the car park there are a series of stepping stones over the river and you can walk across these and then along the creekside path.

Lerryn is a tidal creek where the River Lerryn joins the River Fowey. It used to be an active river port, when stream-fed mills ground corn higher in the valley. Now it is a beautifully tranquil oasis visited by few. Perhaps the best way – for me – would be to arrive by boat, as I did many years ago at the top of a spring tide, from Fowey. It was a sunlit September afternoon and the journey was pure magic; more 'Tales of the Riverbank' than Poldark, but no less worth doing.

On the day we did this walk there was no wind, providing perfect mirror images of the houses and boats on the glass-like water, and the only sounds were the odd seagull and the persistent whine of a chainsaw at work in the woods. We continued along this tarmac path, past a row of cottages, until we reached Ethy Woods. During the late 1990s, many interesting lichen were found in Ethy Woods, and in 2013 a species new to England was found. These woods also inspired Kenneth Grahame to write the chapter about the Wild Woods in *Wind in the Willows*.

Stepping stones, Lerryn

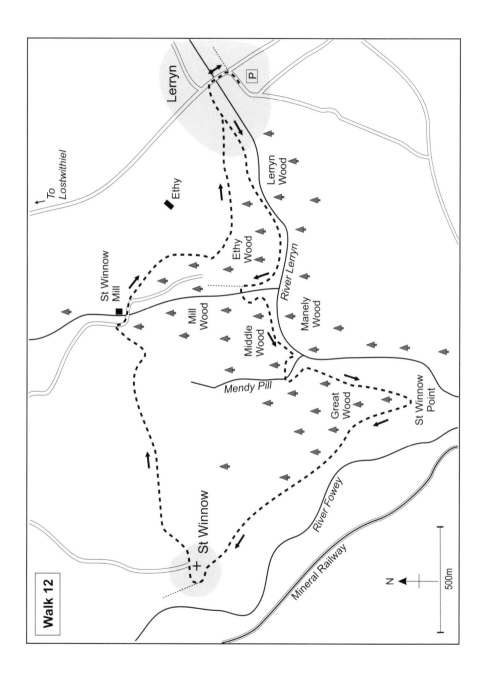

Walk 12

Lerryn

To Lostwithiel

Ethy

St Winnow Mill

Ethy Wood

Lerryn Wood

River Lerryn

Mill Wood

Middle Wood

Manely Wood

Mendy Pill

Great Wood

St Winnow Point

St Winnow

River Fowey

Mineral Railway

N

500m

P

Lerryn

Walking through these woods was the embodiment of peace and stillness, bar the odd ripple of a fish surfacing, a mallard flying by, and the distant rush of water. Old trees have toppled into the river Lerryn and lie part submerged, like strange prehistoric creatures of the deep. The woods are a mixture of young holly trees and very old oak trees, with small emerald ferns peeking from the branches that spread gracefully from the wide, solid trunks covered in a rich bright green moss, like a soft duvet.

The path winds inland along a small inlet – there are hundreds of little twisty paths through the gorse and heather here. Long tendrils of moss hung from various branches while an oyster catcher called in the distance. We turned left at a waymark sign, with a large reedy area on the opposite bank. This path led along a muddy stretch, over slate steps and some boardwalks which cross the stream to lead round the opposite side of the river back towards the creek. Rhododendron bushes grow along the creek side of the path, and more holly trees, and several small beech trees with copper coloured leaves still clinging on.

This path continued above Lerryn Creek until we turned left onto a wide gravel track, then after a short while came to a yellow waymark sign with a blue circle leading back onto the woodland path. We crossed a fast flowing stream then continued, skirting a small inlet known as Mendy Pill, while the path beneath our feet was covered in leaves of myriad shades, from conker brown, reddish hues, orange and ochre yellow, interspersed with fragments of fallen lichen of the palest green.

Heading up some wooden steps by a waymark sign, we headed back onto the gravel track and continued until it gradually narrowed and petered out, leading away from St Winnow Point towards St Winnow itself. Along the creek we came to a few wooden steps, then over a stile we turned left and crossed several fields and stiles, still walking alongside the creek. The roofs of houses and tips of boat masts at St Winnow appeared on our right, while the sky cleared to a pale blue and we reflected how beautiful this would look in spring, studded with primroses' cheerful faces, and nodding bluebells.

Crossing another stile, over a boardwalk across a stream, we reached the foreshore and, as the tide was low, we were able to walk towards St Winnow. If the tide is high, there is a path up on the right where a sign says 'Beware of Bull!' and leads into a field.

The river Fowey lay before us, wide and welcoming, tranquil and secret. On the opposite shore we nearly missed seeing a tiny boathouse, for it blended perfectly into the trees. A few boats were moored in the river, but the only other inhabitants were a gull swooping overhead, and a cormorant, dark neck darting and twisting in search of fish.

Coming to a thoughtfully provided wooden seat, with the inscription 'Lady Jane 2003', we sat and ate our lunch, feeling honoured to be able to watch the oyster catchers pecking around in the mud, and the tree skeletons on the skyline, reminiscent of Rowland Hilder paintings, while dense woods lurked on the opposite shore, giving an almost misty appearance.

Suitably refreshed, we turned right past a converted boathouse and then a boatyard with plenty of boats laid up, and St Winnow Church on our right. Fiona had a friend who had married at this delightfully romantic spot, and it was easy to imagine the wedding of Dwight Enys and Caroline Penvenen, which was used as one of the highlights of the second 1970s TV series, for all the main members of the cast were there.

Boathouse reflection

This quiet church lends itself to joyous occasions, with its beautiful views down the river Fowey, and the wide expanse of open churchyard. This 12th century church, with two large perpendicular tracery windows facing east, and a castellated tower, was substantially rebuilt in the 15th century, and may have been on the site of a Celtic monastery. The north wall is the only remaining part of the original 12th century building. Inside are a collection of carved bench ends from the 15th and 16th century, including a ship in a storm, a man in a Cornish kilt drinking cider, and a St Catherine's Wheel.

Fiona told me about her friend's wedding here – she has understandably fond memories of the church – and as we strolled around the churchyard, I noticed a black and tan cat perched on top of a grave: who else but a cat would manage to doze contentedly on a ledge of about two inches of granite? It watched Moll for several minutes before elegantly yawning, jumping off and disappearing through the hedge.

We left the churchyard via the top gate, which was decorated with holly, and headed uphill, past a clump of snowdrops and grape hyacinth, and turned

St Winnow church

right along a Public Footpath sign by a house on the right. This led along a muddy path to a metal gate, followed by a wide track leading uphill past a little shepherd's hut to a further gate. I struggled to open this gate: "does it need lifting?" suggested Fiona. "Put your back into it!" as it yielded and we headed uphill again through a field. At the end of this field we found a waymark sign and crossed a stile beside a gate, walking diagonally across the field to a stile in the right hand corner.

From here there are wonderful views along the river Fowey and St Winnow – the wide expanse of river winding its way through the silent countryside to the little church nestled in a dip with unusually dense woodlands to the left and right. It's a long time since I've done such a peaceful walk.

At the top of the field we climbed over the stile and walked along the left hand boundary of the field. This led to a waymark sign by a stile and gate from where we walked diagonally right across another field. We came to another stile by a gate and from here we walked diagonally, half left, towards a wooded area.

From here we climbed over two adjacent stiles and followed the left hand boundary of the field, over another stile and into a field where we followed the right hand boundary for a little while, heading steeply downhill, before climbing over a stile on our right. There were cattle in this field so keep dogs on a lead. Over the stile we climbed down some steps and turned right, down a few more wooden steps and onto a gravelled track.

We were back in Ethy Woods now, and turned left where the track divides to pass the remains of St Winnow's Mill. The main path goes straight ahead but we turned left up through the woods, climbing steeply up a path of oak leaves, slate and rocks. Coming to a junction we continued upwards through the trees which brought us to a small gate leading into parkland.

This is National Trust land, and we walked across this elegant park with noble, ancient oak trees and the beautiful Georgian manor house of Ethy on our left. With the silence broken by the incredibly loud tapping of a woodpecker, and the buzz of chainsaws in the dense woods on our right, we followed the waymark signs, came to a five barred gate and could see a path following the left hand boundary of the field. Another path led down the middle of the field so we headed down there, towards some houses and this led to a small cul-de-sac where we turned almost immediately right into the woods once more.

We followed a meandering path (don't turn left) straight on through the pine trees of Ethy Woods, through a gate and across a field that led us back into the woods where we turned first left back onto the lower path and retraced our footsteps of earlier.

Walking back at high tide, the river was incredibly still and Lerryn was reflected like a mystical hamlet in the water. Passing over the small granite bridge back into Lerryn, we encountered another cat – this time a large ginger tom, perched on the side of the bridge, glaring angrily at Moll for disrupting its peace. We had to laugh – Moll was oblivious – then headed towards the Lerryn River Stores where they will provide a hot drink if you wish to sit outside on the lovely grassy area with thoughtfully provided benches. The Ship Inn was shut in the afternoon being winter, but check times in the summer.

Standing looking down the river, we imagined walking here in spring or summer, and having a lovely picnic half way round, sitting on the grass among bluebells or daisies, maybe having a drink in Lerryn before heading home. Actually, this walk would be a joy at any time of the year.

Come here and drink in the peace and serenity of St Winnow church: imagine the joy and bustle of a happy wedding there, then walk quietly back through the fields, enjoying the contrast of the creeks and the parkland, as Ross and Demelza would have done, on their way home.

Also from Sigma Leisure:

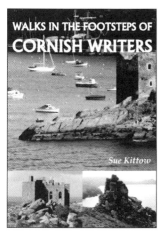

Walks in the Footsteps of Cornish Writers
Sue Kittow

A fascinating insight to contemporary authors and their favourite walks as well as the places that were so special to those well known writers who are no longer with us - and why they were so special. From Derek Tangye's books based in Lamorna to the Reverend Stephen Hawker at Morwenstow, here are a variety of walks that inspired the authors, and it is hoped will inspire readers too.Each walk has an introduction, a factbox with all essential information, and details of maps, refreshments, history, points of interest and clear directions.
£8.99

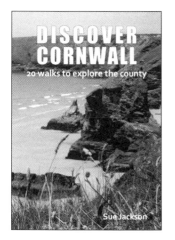

Discover Cornwall
20 walks to explore the county
Sue Kittow

Cornwall's fine golden sands have provided the backdrop for many childhood holidays, but it is also a coastal footpath, there are numerous less known routes that are great fun to investigate. There are a good range of gentle to moderate walks between 4 and 6 miles in length. Discover Cornwall lists 20 walks providing a healthy and entertaining way to keep fit, learn about Cornwall, and enjoy the beaches, moorland and hisotry of this magical county. The walks have clear directions, delightful details and excellent photographs, maing this a unique book to keep and pore over for readers as well as walkers.
£8.99

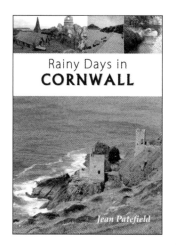

Rainy Days in Cornwall
Jean Patefield

Cornwall has a long and beautiful coastline, with wonderful beaches many of which are excellent for surfing. There are also picturesque valleys and woodland. Overall it merits its place as the premier summer resort in Britain.Unfortunately, being in the west of England, even in high summer wind and rain can lash the beaches, the temperature can plummet and the coast can be shrouded in mist and drizzle. What should one do when your week's summer holiday is turning into a disaster? Carry on regardless, huddled behind a windbreak trying to keep warm or patronise the numerous attractions and spend a fortune? Rainy Days in Cornwall offers a solution to this problem with twenty suggestions of free and interesting things to do in Cornwall in less than perfect weather.

£8.99

Cornwall Walking on the level
Norman & June Buckley

This book selects and illustrates 28 routes, mainly circular, which explore some of the finest parts of the county, without serious ascent. In addition to the route directions, the distance, ascent, car parking, refreshment and map, with a succinct assessment, are provided for each walk.

£8.99

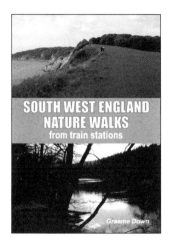

South West England Nature Walks
from train stations
Graeme Down

Get away from it all and find nature using the train! Although the countryside is easily accessible by car, it's far more relaxing to combine the beauty of the countryside with the less stressful mode of train travel. 24 circular walks, two walks for each month of the year, timed to give maximum chance of spotting the wildlife on offer. Each route is clearly described and accompanied by a map. Along the way, hints are given to help the reader identify some of the wildlife they may be able to find.
£8.99

Dorset Accessible Walks
25 accessible walks in the beautiful county of Dorset
Marie Houlden

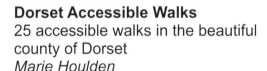

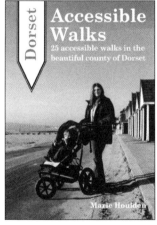

For each walk there is a brief description and then more detailed information about distance, gradient and terrain, allowing the reader to make an informed decision about the suitability of their equipment and their own particular needs. All of the walks are stile and obstacle free, with consideration given to those in wheelchairs, including information on disabled parking spots and accessible facilities. With walks that start from only a mile and that cover a mixture of terrain and environments, there really is something for everyone. There are even a couple of more strenuous walks for those with an all-terrain pushchair and a passion for a physical challenge!
£8.99

Walking in and around Hampshire's Meon Valley
Louis Murray

The river Meon is one of Hampshire's quintessential chalk streams. It rises from natural springs in the South Downs to the south of the village of East Meon. This book contains the details of 20 walks in the Meon river valley area in southern Hampshire. The walks are suitable for novices, casual walkers, family groups, and experienced ramblers.
£8.99

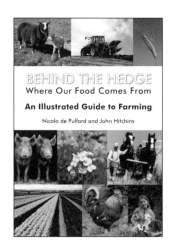

Behind the Hedge
Where Our Food Comes From
An Illustrated Guide to Farming
Nicola de Paulford & John Hitchins

For everyone who wants to know more about the food we eat, the land it is grown and reared on, and those who farm it. This fully illustrated easy-to-follow colour guide will help you identify in their natural environment our crops, fruit and farm animals, agricultural buildings and machinery, the farming landscape and the wildlife it supports. Never again will you mistake a field of wheat for one of barley, or an Aberdeen Angus cow for a Hereford. .
£12.99

All of our books are all available on-line at **www.sigmapress.co.uk** or through booksellers. For a free catalogue, please contact:

Sigma Leisure, Stobart House, Pontyclerc, Penybanc Road, Ammanford, Carmarthenshire SA18 3HP
Tel: 01269 593100   Fax: 01269 596116
info@sigmapress.co.uk   www.sigmapress.co.uk